LET HER DIE WORKBOOK

MELISSA DEAN

MAGICSEEKER HOUSE

Journey Markers

WELCOME TO THE WORK

This isn't just paper.

This is the mirror you've been avoiding and I wanted it to mirror the book.

The one that reflects back the version of you who's been buried under everyone else's expectations, your own doubts, and the quiet stories you tell yourself when no one's listening.

If you've read *Let Her Die*, you already know... we're not here to play small, stay polite, or wait for perfect timing. This workbook is where those pages turn into action. It's where you stop just nodding along and start moving the pen across the page, carving out your truth in ink.

You're going to see questions in here that make you pause. Some will punch you right in the gut. Some will feel so obvious, you'll wonder why you've never answered them before. Answer anyway. Even if your brain tells you it's "too much" or "not important."

These pages are for *you*... not for an audience, not for the highlight reel, not for anyone else's approval. Be raw here. Be honest. Let yourself write the things you wouldn't say out loud yet.

By the time you finish, you won't just be reading about letting her die, you'll be standing in the bones of who you used to be, holding space for the woman you've been becoming all along.

Welcome to the work.

Let's kill the version of you that keeps you small.

How to Use This Workbook

At the start of each section, you'll see the same questions and reflections that appear in the matching chapter of *Let Her Die*.

These are here so you can work through the book without having to flip back and forth — and so you can see your answers all in one place.

From there, we'll go deeper.

You'll find **additional prompts** that aren't in the main book — questions to push you further, dig under the surface, and help you connect the dots between what you've read and what you're ready to change.

The only rule? **Be honest.**

This isn't for anyone else's eyes. Let the words spill.

WHY THIS WORKBOOK MATCHES THE BOOK

I intentionally chose to make this workbook (almost) the same size and style as *Let Her Die* for a reason.

When you put them side by side, I want you to see more than similar sizes... I want you to see a conversation.

The book holds my story.
This workbook will hold yours.

Page by page, you'll be writing your own version of *Let Her Die*... your own moments of awareness, your own ego battles, your own turning points where you finally said, "Not anymore.

By the time you're done, your workbook will be just as full as my book... not with my words, but with your truth.

That's the point.

Because this isn't just about reading my journey... it's about writing yours.

First things first. **A letter to yourself.** Before you dive into these pages, I want you to meet yourself right here, exactly as you are today. This isn't the version you're working toward or the version you *wish* you were.

This one.

The one sitting here, holding this book, maybe feeling hopeful, maybe feeling scared, maybe not even sure why you bought it.

Write to her.

Tell her what brought you here. Tell her what you want from this journey, even if it's messy or unsure. Tell her what you hope she remembers when the ego gets loud, or when the old stories start creeping back in.

You don't have to get it "right." This letter is not for anyone else's eyes. It's for the future you — the one who will read it when these pages are full and think, *Damn... I've come a long way.*

Start with "Hey Beautiful..." and let it flow.

_____
_____
_____
_____
_____
_____
_____
_____
_____
_____
_____
_____
_____
_____
_____
_____
_____
_____
_____
_____

Now, re-read what you wrote. Sit with it for a moment. Really see where you're at. Were you brutally honest? Are there any parts where you could be more honest with yourself? Remember, this is just for you. You don't have to put up any fronts. If there's anything you'd like to add, now is the time. Thank you for being here. Thank you for showing up for you. This is the beginning of a beautifully, messy journey.

Chapter 1
Identifying Your Ego

IDENTIFYING YOUR EGO

You've met her before... the voice that doesn't yell, but knows exactly where to press. She isn't just arrogance, she's that steady, familiar whisper that says you're not ready, not qualified, not enough. She dresses up like logic. She wraps herself in concern. She offers you comfort only when you're on the edge of something brave.

Remember, Ego's not the villain, she's scared. She's in protection and preservation mode. She wants to keep you safe in the room you've outgrown. But safety at the cost of growth is just self-abandonment in a prettier outfit.

This chapter is about learning to spot her. Naming her. Talking back. Thanking her for the protection, but reminding her she doesn't get to run the show anymore.

Journal Prompts (from the book):
What does your ego actually sound like? What are her go-to lines? Her favorite excuses?

_____
_____
_____
_____
_____
_____
_____
_____
_____
_____
_____
_____
_____

_____
_____
_____
_____
_____
_____

What fear is she trying to protect you from? (And does it even belong to you?)

_____
_____
_____
_____
_____
_____
_____
_____
_____
_____
_____
_____
_____
_____

Where do you feel her in your body? What shifts when she's calling the shots?

_____
_____
_____
_____
_____
_____
_____
_____
_____
_____
_____
_____
_____
_____

What would it look like to thank her... and do the thing anyway?

_____
_____
_____
_____
_____
_____
_____
_____
_____
_____
_____
_____
_____
_____
_____
_____

What's one old tape she keeps replaying... and what new truth are you ready to replace it with?

_____
_____
_____
_____
_____
_____
_____
_____
_____
_____
_____
_____
_____
_____
_____
_____

What's something brave she tried to stop, but you did it anyway? How did that feel?

_____
_____
_____

_____
_____
_____
_____
_____
_____
_____
_____
_____
_____
_____
_____

Are you living in the room you've outgrown... or the one you've been waiting for?

_____
_____
_____
_____
_____
_____
_____
_____
_____
_____
_____
_____
_____
_____
_____

A few more I'd like you to think about. *(These go beyond the book to deepen the work.)*

Think of a moment where ego dressed up as logic. What did she say to convince you?

_____
_____
_____
_____
_____
_____

_____
_____
_____
_____
_____
_____
_____
_____
_____
_____

When you imagine your "Room One" and "Room Two," where do you spend most of your time? What does each feel like in your body?

Room 1

_____
_____
_____
_____
_____
_____
_____
_____
_____
_____

Room 2

_____
_____
_____
_____
_____
_____
_____
_____
_____
_____
_____

When you hear yourself procrastinating, doubting, or "waiting until it's perfect"... what might ego be trying to protect?

_____
_____
_____
_____
_____
_____
_____
_____
_____
_____
_____
_____

Describe a recent situation where your ego got loud. What triggered her? How did you respond?

_____
_____
_____
_____
_____
_____
_____

_____
_____
_____
_____
_____
_____
_____
_____

If your ego had a physical form (person, creature, object), what would she look like? What does her posture, expression, or energy say about her role in your life?

_____
_____
_____
_____
_____
_____
_____
_____
_____
_____
_____
_____
_____
_____
_____
_____

Write a short letter to your ego thanking her for what she's tried to protect you from — then telling her what's about to change.

_____
_____
_____
_____
_____
_____
_____
_____
_____
_____
_____

_____
_____
_____
_____

Think of a time when your ego was quiet and you felt completely in your power. What was different in your environment, your thoughts, or your body?

_____
_____
_____
_____
_____
_____
_____
_____
_____
_____
_____
_____
_____
_____
_____
_____

Finish this sentence five times:
I hear you, Ego, but I'm doing it anyway because

I hear you, Ego, but I'm doing it anyway because

I hear you, Ego, but I'm doing it anyway because

I hear you, Ego, but I'm doing it anyway because

I hear you, Ego, but I'm doing it anyway because

Create a personal mantra for when ego shows up... short enough to remember in the moment, but strong enough to pull you back to yourself:

Self-Awareness Inventory:

Fill in the blanks...

My ego's tone is: □ harsh □ condescending □ comforting □ anxious □ passive-aggressive □ something else: _____

Her favorite disguise is: □ logic □ self-care □ protection □ humility □ over-preparation □ something else: _____

When she's running the show, I feel: □ frozen □ overwhelmed □ avoidant □ small □ all of the above

I'm ready to be:
□
□
□
□
□

Rewrite the Script:

Pick one old belief or ego line and rewrite it with your truth.

Old script: *"I'm not ready for this."*
New truth: *"Readiness is a myth. I'm moving forward anyway."*

Old script:
New truth:

Real Life Challenge:

Say one thing out loud this week that your ego doesn't want you to say. Post something. Ask for help. Hit send. Start anyway.
I decided I'm going to:

_____

Then journal: *How did it feel afterward?*

_____

———————————————————————————
———————————————————————————
———————————————————————————
———————————————————————————
———————————————————————————
———————————————————————————
———————————————————————————
———————————————————————————
———————————————————————————
———————————————————————————
———————————————————————————
———————————————————————————
———————————————————————————
———————————————————————————

By now, you realize, your ego isn't here to destroy you... she's here to keep you safe. But safety without growth becomes a cage. Every time you thank her and still choose the braver path, you're proving that you can hold both courage and care for yourself at the same time

Bonus Affirmation:

"I see you, ego. But I choose alignment over safety."

Doodle other affirmations here:

Chapter 2
We Don't Do That Anymore

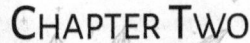

CHAPTER TWO

WE DON'T DO THAT ANYMORE

Change doesn't fail because we're weak... it feels hard because we're wired to repeat. We keep dancing to old rhythms, even when they don't fit us anymore, because they're familiar. That includes the quiet, constant habit of tearing ourselves down.

Sometimes we don't even notice when the voice in our head isn't ours. It's layered, you know, the magazine covers, offhand comments, old insults, all stitched together over years until it sounds like truth. That's the problem with familiarity: it can masquerade as reality.

This chapter is about breaking that trance. About calling out the programming, catching it mid-sentence, and drawing a line in the sand with one simple phrase: *We don't do that anymore.* Not as a Pinterest affirmation, but as a boundary. It's a shift. A declaration that you're not playing by the same rules anymore.

Here's where you practice it.

What version of self-talk do I want my kids (or future kids) to internalize from watching me? *What would I hope they say to themselves one day when they look in the mirror?*

_____
_____
_____
_____
_____
_____
_____
_____
_____
_____
_____
_____
_____
_____
_____
_____
_____
_____
_____
_____

What messages did I receive growing up that I now recognize were harmful—even if they were unintentional? *What am I still carrying that it's time to release?*

_____
_____
_____
_____
_____
_____
_____
_____
_____
_____
_____
_____
_____
_____
_____
_____
_____
_____

Whose voice is still lingering in my head—and does that person deserve to live rent-free in my mind anymore?

_____
_____
_____
_____
_____
_____
_____
_____
_____
_____
_____
_____
_____
_____
_____
_____
_____
_____

What does being a cycle-breaker look like for me? *What beliefs, patterns, or behaviors stop with me?*

_____
_____
_____
_____
_____
_____
_____
_____
_____
_____
_____
_____
_____
_____
_____
_____
_____
_____
_____

If my child spoke to themselves the way I sometimes speak to myself... how would I respond?

_____
_____
_____
_____
_____
_____
_____
_____
_____
_____
_____
_____
_____
_____
_____
_____
_____

What's one belief I've repeated to myself that no longer feels true, but still shows up like it's mine?

_____
_____
_____
_____
_____
_____
_____
_____
_____
_____
_____
_____
_____
_____
_____
_____

Where did I first learn to be critical of myself? Was it a person, a moment, or a pattern?

_____
_____
_____
_____
_____
_____
_____
_____
_____
_____
_____
_____
_____
_____
_____
_____
_____
_____

What would it feel like to believe I am enough *without* conditions?

_____
_____
_____
_____
_____
_____
_____
_____
_____
_____
_____
_____
_____
_____
_____
_____

What are three things I would never say to a friend, but often say to myself? (or if you heard a friend speaking to herself that way, how would you react?)

_____

_____
_____
_____
_____
_____
_____
_____
_____
_____
_____
_____
_____
_____
_____
_____
_____

When my inner critic shows up, what does she sound like? What does she want me to believe?

_____
_____
_____
_____
_____
_____
_____
_____
_____
_____
_____
_____
_____
_____
_____
_____

How does my body respond when I speak kindly to it? How does it respond when I don't?

_____
_____

_____
_____
_____
_____
_____
_____
_____
_____
_____
_____
_____
_____
_____

What does "we don't do that anymore" mean to me right now? What thought, behavior, or pattern am I ready to interrupt?

_____
_____
_____
_____
_____
_____
_____
_____
_____
_____
_____
_____
_____
_____
_____

Is this thought true or is it just familiar?

_____
_____
_____

_____
_____
_____
_____
_____
_____
_____
_____
_____
_____
_____
_____

What recurring thought or behavior am I ready to interrupt starting today?

_____
_____
_____
_____
_____
_____
_____
_____
_____
_____
_____
_____
_____
_____
_____
_____

What is one way I can set a boundary with myself when old patterns show up? Explain:

_____
_____
_____
_____
_____

_____
_____
_____
_____
_____
_____
_____
_____
_____
_____
_____
_____

Whose opinion am I still carrying that I'm ready to let go of? Why?

_____
_____
_____
_____
_____
_____
_____
_____
_____
_____
_____
_____
_____
_____
_____
_____
_____
_____

What would it look like to embody "we don't do that anymore" in how I speak, how I move, and how I make decisions?

_____
_____
_____
_____
_____

_____
_____
_____
_____
_____
_____
_____
_____
_____
_____
_____
_____
_____
_____
_____
_____
_____
_____
_____
_____
_____
_____
_____
_____
_____
_____
_____
_____

Mirror Work: The Moment of Recognition

Write down a few common things you say to yourself when you look in the mirror (or think about your appearance or worth).

-
-
-

Where do you think these voices came from? (Be honest—was it a comment, a cultural message, a memory, a moment?)

-
-
-

The Interruption: Practicing "We Don't Do That Anymore"
Practice Exercise:
Next time a negative thought arises, speak this phrase out loud or in your head:

"We don't do that anymore."

Then, write the thought below. Cross it out. Underneath, write what you're choosing instead.

Old Thought:

New Thought:

example: Old Thought: "You're so lazy."
New Thought: "We don't do that anymore. Rest is not laziness. I'm allowed to pause."

Old Thought:

New Thought:

Old Thought:

New Thought:

Repeat this any time the critic creeps in. It's all about awareness.

Who's Really Talking?

Who does your inner critic sound like? (Name a few people, messages, or moments.)

-

-

-

Do you still respect or believe these people/messages? If not, why are they still allowed to shape your self-perception?

-

-

-

Write one sentence you're ready to reclaim right now. Turn the old belief into a new truth.

Old Belief:

New Truth: *We don't do that anymore. Instead, I believe*

What messages did you receive growing up that you now recognize were harmful...even if they were meant well?

-
-
-

Now knowing what you know, what cycle stops with you?

-
-
-

What are some things you didn't realize were holding you back:

-
-
-

Every time you say, *We don't do that anymore*, you're reclaiming space inside yourself. You're not just breaking a habit... you're building a home where your truth feels safe to live. Keep practicing until this voice feels more natural than the one you're replacing. You've got this. And when all else fails: We don't do that anymore. I am beautiful. I am worthy. I am enough.

Let Her Die

```
                              U V K H B R A V E A
                            E P R A O O W C N A
                          M J Y E C S Y S L
                          V D A S G U H E
                        X B U P T U R T I
                      D A U O E Z R R R
                    G M A G I C E O A E
                  G R O W T H N W D C H
                  O C A E D D T N Y A
                T N E X J E K U U P D
              B K U X N R S O E P V
              L O V E V O B E Y S E
            Y K C F E G K U M S O F
            C Y H G Q C B O G V U Y
            Y O L Z F J N N V H N
          Q J Q D P H E G M I W D
          L A E H C Y D V C D P T
          B E C O M I N G L V L R
          E V O L F L E S N S A A
          M A N T R A S T R O Y C
          M I N D F U L H N U F K
          L E T H E R D I E L U P
          U T Y A D Y E R G W L T
          E S R E V I N U R O N S
          X B I C J Y F T J R E K
          Z U F K K T F G K S M
          Y N Y G R E N E R S R
          R T N E M N G I L A Q M
          L X J W T T Z S V X X
          H A M O S B B Y I X Y
          F A Z U C O U R A G E
          Q D Q R R R N K D P J
          L K T Q N W O B X F D
          E Y S V E G I D B E
          C X U H Y P T T N M
          T U L K J C A S J A
          T E V S G A R H O
          H T U R T B W Y S
            S I T C I M O G E T
            S C V Q E C A E P Z
```

WORD LIST

ALIGNMENT	GREY DAY	MAGIC	SOUNDTRACK
BECOMING	GROWTH	MANTRAS	SURRENDER
BOUNDARIES	HAPPY MONEY	MINDFUL	TRUST
BRAVE	HEAL	PEACE	TRUTH
COURAGE	JOURNEY	PLAYFULNESS	UNIVERSE
EGO	JOY	REST	VIBRATION
ENERGY	LET HER DIE	SELF LOVE	WORTHY
ENOUGH	LOVE	SOUL WORK	

YOUR ORACLE
PULL

Pick a number that calls to you.
Flip to the back to reveal your message.

Chapter 3
Was That Helpful

CHAPTER THREE

WAS THAT HELPFUL

S pirals are sneaky. One second you're answering emails, making lunches, getting gas... the next, your brain is whispering sweet nothings like: "You're a failure." "You're behind." "Everyone's doing better than you." But here's the shift: you pause and ask one thing..."Is this helpful?"

That's it. Not "Am I right?" Not "How do I fix this?" Just... is this helpful? It's the quiet, neutral voice in the corner of your mind that's not judging, just curious. And it has the power to interrupt the shame loop, the burnout loop, the over-functioning loop... all of it.

Shame tries to convince you that you *are* the problem, not that you're having a problem. But when you pause and listen, you realize it's often a sign that something's misaligned with your real values. That's not the moment to beat yourself up, it's the moment to check in, adjust, and choose a different response.

This is where we work on catching yourself mid-spiral, using the question "Is this helpful?" as your handrail, and turning around before you reach the bottom of the staircase.

What does your inner spiral look like? How does it show up in your body, your thoughts, your habits?

_____
_____
_____
_____
_____
_____
_____
_____
_____
_____
_____
_____
_____
_____
_____
_____
_____
_____

When was the last time you asked yourself, "Is this helpful?" What did you find?

_____
_____
_____
_____
_____
_____
_____
_____
_____
_____
_____
_____
_____
_____
_____
_____
_____
_____

What were you doing, thinking, or believing today that might seem productive but is actually keeping you stuck?

_____
_____
_____
_____
_____
_____
_____
_____
_____
_____
_____
_____
_____
_____
_____
_____
_____
_____

What would it look like to choose gentleness instead of judgment when you catch yourself in a spiral?

_____
_____
_____
_____
_____
_____
_____
_____
_____
_____
_____
_____
_____
_____
_____
_____
_____
_____

What tiny shift could you make today that would help you feel 5% more grounded?

_____
_____
_____
_____
_____
_____
_____
_____
_____
_____
_____
_____
_____
_____
_____
_____
_____
_____
_____

What's my personal "spiral staircase"... the sequence of thoughts or actions that pull me down?

_____
_____
_____
_____
_____
_____

_____
_____
_____
_____
_____
_____
_____
_____
_____
_____
_____

What are my early warning signs that I'm entering a spiral? (Physical, emotional, behavioral)

_____
_____
_____
_____
_____
_____
_____
_____
_____
_____
_____
_____
_____
_____
_____
_____

Who in my life can help me spot a spiral when I can't see it?

_____
_____
_____
_____
_____
_____

_____

_____

_____

What's one "rest practice" I can choose next time I catch the spiral starting?

_____

_____

_____

_____

_____

_____

_____

_____

_____

_____

_____

_____

_____

_____

_____

_____

How do I want to talk to myself in the moment I pause? Write the exact words.

_____

_____

_____

_____

_____

_____

_____

_____

_____

_____

_____

_____

_____

_____

_____

_____

What's your default spiral behavior?
☐ Over-explaining   ☐ Cleaning frenzy
☐ Checking emails 40 times   ☐ Shutting down
☐ Snapping at people   ☐ Saying "I'm fine" (when you're not)
☐ Other: _____

Doodle Break: Doodle your baseline (words that describe when you feel most "you")
This can be emotional, physical, or mental "signs" of when you feel grounded

What are 3 triggers that *pull you away* from that baseline? (Situations, people, thoughts, expectations, etc.)
1.

2.

3.

SHAME CHECKPOINT:

We're not here to shame shame—we're here to listen to what it's trying to tell you.

Have you felt shame recently?
If yes, what did it say about *you*...and what might it *really* be pointing to underneath?
Example: "You're lazy" → Maybe I haven't rested in weeks.

_____
_____

_____

_____

_____

_____

_____

What value of yours did this moment *not align with*? *(e.g., I value presence, but I was rushing and snapping all day)*

_____

_____

_____

_____

_____

_____

_____

_____

_____

_____

If you could offer yourself gentleness right now, what would it sound like? *Write yourself one compassionate sentence as if talking to a best friend.*

_____

_____

_____

_____

_____

This question isn't magic, but it is a crack in the wall. Every time you ask "Is this helpful?" you're building the muscle of self-awareness. That's where change begins. The goal isn't to never spiral again (trust me...you WILL spiral again) it's to notice sooner, pause longer, and choose better. One step back toward yourself at a time.

Reminder: *"Awareness isn't a finish line. It's a flashlight. You use it to see where you are, not shame where you've been."*

Every time you pause, you rewrite the pattern.

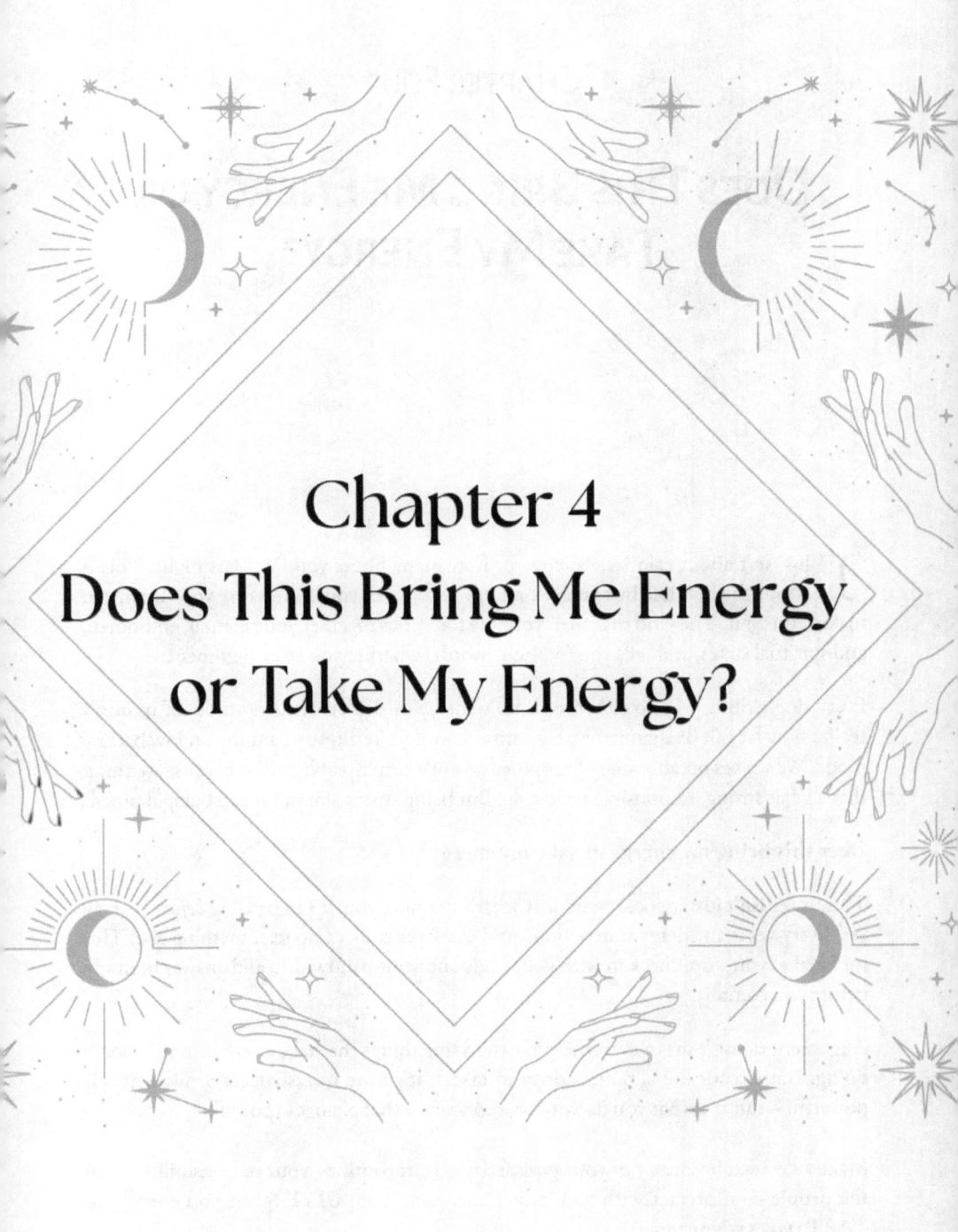

Chapter 4
Does This Bring Me Energy or Take My Energy?

CHAPTER FOUR

DOES THIS BRING ME ENERGY OR TAKE MY ENERGY?

This isn't about calories, caffeine, or how many hours you slept last night. This is about the invisible but tangible energy you feel in your gut before your brain can make sense of it. The kind that fuels your life force, ties together your mental, emotional, and spiritual states, and tells you (without words) whether you're in alignment.

Every single thing you do either feeds that energy or depletes it. And most of us don't realize how far out of alignment we've drifted until we're already running on low battery mode. We say yes because we're "supposed" to. We keep up obligations because we think that's what strong, responsible people do. But being strong doesn't mean being drained.

Does this bring me energy or take my energy?

The power isn't just in looking back at what's draining you, it's in pausing *before* you say yes. Every yes is an energy transaction. And every yes is also a no to something else. This tool makes you stop, check in with your body and your bandwidth, and answer honestly before you commit.

Alignment doesn't mean everything is easy. Some things that take energy are still worth doing. But if your life is built mostly of takers, it's time to restructure. Awareness is powerful—but it's what you do with that awareness that changes your life.

Make a detailed inventory of your typical day—your routines, your responsibilities, and the people you interact with regularly. Label each item: **GIVE** (gives you energy) or **TAKE** (takes your energy).

Which items surprised you when you labeled them?

_____
_____
_____
_____
_____
_____
_____
_____
_____
_____
_____
_____
_____
_____
_____
_____
_____
_____

What's one "TAKE" you're ready to release or adjust this week? Why?

_____
_____
_____
_____
_____
_____
_____
_____
_____
_____
_____
_____
_____
_____
_____
_____
_____
_____
_____
_____

What's one "GIVE" you can add or make more space for?

_____
_____
_____
_____
_____
_____
_____
_____
_____
_____
_____
_____
_____
_____
_____
_____
_____
_____

How does your body respond when you imagine removing one of your biggest "TAKE" items?

_____
_____
_____
_____
_____
_____
_____
_____
_____
_____

_____
_____
_____
_____
_____
_____

Which people in your life consistently give you energy? How can you nurture those relationships?

_____
_____
_____
_____
_____
_____
_____
_____
_____
_____
_____
_____
_____
_____
_____
_____
_____
_____

Where in your life do you need to set clearer boundaries to protect your energy?

_____
_____
_____
_____
_____
_____
_____
_____
_____
_____
_____
_____
_____

_____
_____
_____
_____

If you asked "Does this give me energy or take it?" before saying yes to anything for the next 30 days, what do you think would change?

_____
_____
_____
_____
_____
_____
_____
_____
_____
_____
_____
_____
_____
_____
_____
_____
_____

What is one "obligatory yes" I've given recently that I now realize took my energy

_____
_____
_____
_____
_____
_____
_____
_____
_____
_____
_____
_____
_____
_____

_____

_____

Where am I mistaking familiarity for alignment?

_____

_____

_____

_____

_____

_____

_____

_____

_____

_____

_____

_____

_____

_____

_____

Who or what drains my energy the fastest—and why do I keep allowing it?

_____

_____

_____

_____

_____

_____

_____

_____

_____

_____

_____

_____

_____

_____

What rituals or practices consistently refill my energy tank?

_____
_____
_____
_____
_____
_____
_____
_____
_____
_____
_____
_____
_____
_____
_____
_____
_____
_____

How does it feel in my body when something is a true "GIVE"? Be specific.

_____
_____
_____
_____
_____
_____
_____
_____
_____
_____
_____
_____
_____
_____
_____
_____
_____

How can I create a built-in pause before I say yes?

_____
_____

_____

_____

_____

_____

_____

_____

_____

_____

_____

_____

_____

_____

_____

What's one area of my life where I've been over-functioning that I could scale back?

_____

_____

_____

_____

_____

_____

_____

_____

_____

_____

_____

_____

_____

_____

_____

_____

TRUTH CHECK-IN:

Circle any of the following that feel true for you right now:

I say yes to things I don't want to do out of guilt or obligation

I'm operating on autopilot

I feel drained after being around certain people

I've forgotten what lights me up

I miss myself

I mistake being "busy" for being aligned

- What's one thing on your list that *used to* bring you energy but doesn't anymore? Why do you think that changed?
  →

- Who or what feels like they demand more from you than you have to give?
  →

- If your life was based only on things that *fuel* you—what would stay? What would go?
  →

- What would it feel like to move through your day without guilt? Without "shoulds"? Without performance?
  →

Finish the sentence:
I've been keeping this version of me alive because...

ENERGY REFRAME:

Choose 1 item from your **"Takes Energy"** list and answer:

    1. **Why have I kept this in my life?**

    2. **What boundary, change, or support would shift how this feels?**

    3. **Is it time to release this, or reimagine it?**

Your energy is your currency. Spend it on what matters. This tool is about more than time management, it's about *life* management. You don't owe anyone the version of you who runs on fumes. You owe yourself the honesty to check in, the courage to say no, and the intention to choose what truly fuels you. Protecting your energy isn't selfish, not at all, it's how you stay connected to the life you're fighting for.

e journey of becoming

Across

The shift from performing healing to living it

A ritual of money that feels joyful, not pressured

The practice of presence that stops the spiral

The force that invites play and creativity

The practice of speaking kindly to yourself in the mirror

Down

1 The brave decision to stop people-pleasing

2 The filter question: Does this give or take?

4 The Universes way of confirming youre supported

6 The sacred pause that whispers, This isn't working hint* two words

7 Choosing values over money is choosing this

10 The sneaky inner voice that whispers doubt

11 When you say, "We don't do that anymore," you're breaking this

Chapter 5
What Am I Fighting For

CHAPTER FIVE

WHAT AM I FIGHTING FOR?

This isn't a pretty, journal-prompt kind of question. *What am I fighting for* is the rope you grab when the ground feels like it's dropping out from under you.

It's the one I reach for when I catch myself brushing off my kids' stories, snapping too fast, or numbing out in the middle of a moment I actually care about. It's not about a perfect answer, it's about the pause, the second breath. The remembering.

Some days, the fog is too thick to see more than two feet ahead. You're tired. Overstimulated. Doubt is louder than anything you believe in. But asking this question (*even when you don't know the answer*) gives you something solid to hold onto. It pulls you out of autopilot and back into intention.

Your fight might be for your peace, for the woman you're becoming, or simply to make it through the next five minutes without losing yourself. All of those count. And they're all enough.

What is one thing I'm currently fighting for, even if I haven't said it out loud?

_____
_____
_____
_____
_____
_____
_____
_____
_____
_____

_____

_____

_____

_____

_____

_____

_____

What signs does my body give me when I'm off-center?

_____

_____

_____

_____

_____

_____

_____

_____

_____

_____

_____

_____

_____

_____

_____

_____

What's one moment from this week I wish I had paused and asked this question?

_____
_____
_____
_____
_____
_____
_____
_____
_____
_____
_____
_____
_____
_____
_____
_____
_____
_____

What kind of person am I trying to be, and what's worth fighting for in her name?

_____
_____
_____
_____
_____
_____
_____
_____
_____
_____
_____
_____
_____
_____
_____
_____
_____
_____

When I feel overwhelmed, what are my top three "why's" that can bring me back?

_____

_____
_____
_____
_____
_____
_____
_____
_____
_____
_____
_____
_____
_____
_____
_____
_____

Where am I currently fighting battles that don't belong to me?

_____
_____
_____
_____
_____
_____
_____
_____
_____
_____
_____
_____
_____
_____
_____
_____

What is one recurring situation that makes me forget my why—and how can I interrupt it?

_____
_____
_____
_____
_____
_____
_____
_____
_____
_____
_____
_____
_____
_____
_____
_____

Who or what is worth my fight even when it costs me energy?

_____
_____
_____
_____
_____
_____
_____
_____
_____
_____
_____
_____
_____
_____
_____
_____

How does my body physically feel when I'm aligned with my why? How does it feel when I'm not?

_____
_____
_____
_____
_____
_____
_____
_____
_____
_____
_____
_____
_____
_____
_____
_____

What small, daily action could keep my why visible and tangible?

_____
_____
_____
_____
_____
_____
_____
_____
_____
_____
_____
_____
_____
_____
_____
_____

The Cord Visualization

Imagine that colored cord around your wrist.
What's on the other end of it?

□ My kids
□ My peace
□ The healed version of me
□ My freedom
□ My voice
□ My softness
□ My boundaries
□ My dream that won't let go
□ Something else: _____

Draw or write about what that cord looks like. What color is it? What does it feel like to hold onto it? Feel free to doodle here:)

Scene Check

Let's start here—no fluff. You're in it. Your body knows it. Where are you right now?

□ I'm overwhelmed
□ I'm overstimulated
□ I'm shutting down
□ I'm snapping at people I love
□ I'm questioning everything
□ I'm just... tired

Now, take a breath.

Inhale 1...2...3...4
Hold 1...2...3...4
Exhale 1...2...3...4...5...6
Repeat twice.

You're here. You're trying. That counts.

Mini Reset Tools (pick one for your toolbox)

□ Walk barefoot in the grass
□ Stretch your arms overhead and sigh like you mean it
□ Tap (EFT): cross arms and gently tap your biceps
□ Name 3 things you can see, 2 you can touch, 1 you can hear
□ Say: "I'm still in this. I haven't given up."

Doodle Break:)

You won't always have a clear answer and that's okay. The fight isn't always about action; sometimes it's about attention. It's pulling on the cord, even when the fog hasn't lifted yet. You're still in the fight, and that means something. The next time the world gets loud or your own voice turns against you, pause. Breathe. Ask the question. Your why will find you again.

Final Nudge

You don't need to know the full plan. You just need one reason to keep going today. Check your answer:

☐ To show up with more presence
☐ To not pass this pain forward
☐ To remember who I am
☐ To feel like myself again
☐ To become the version of me I haven't met yet

Or write your own: _____

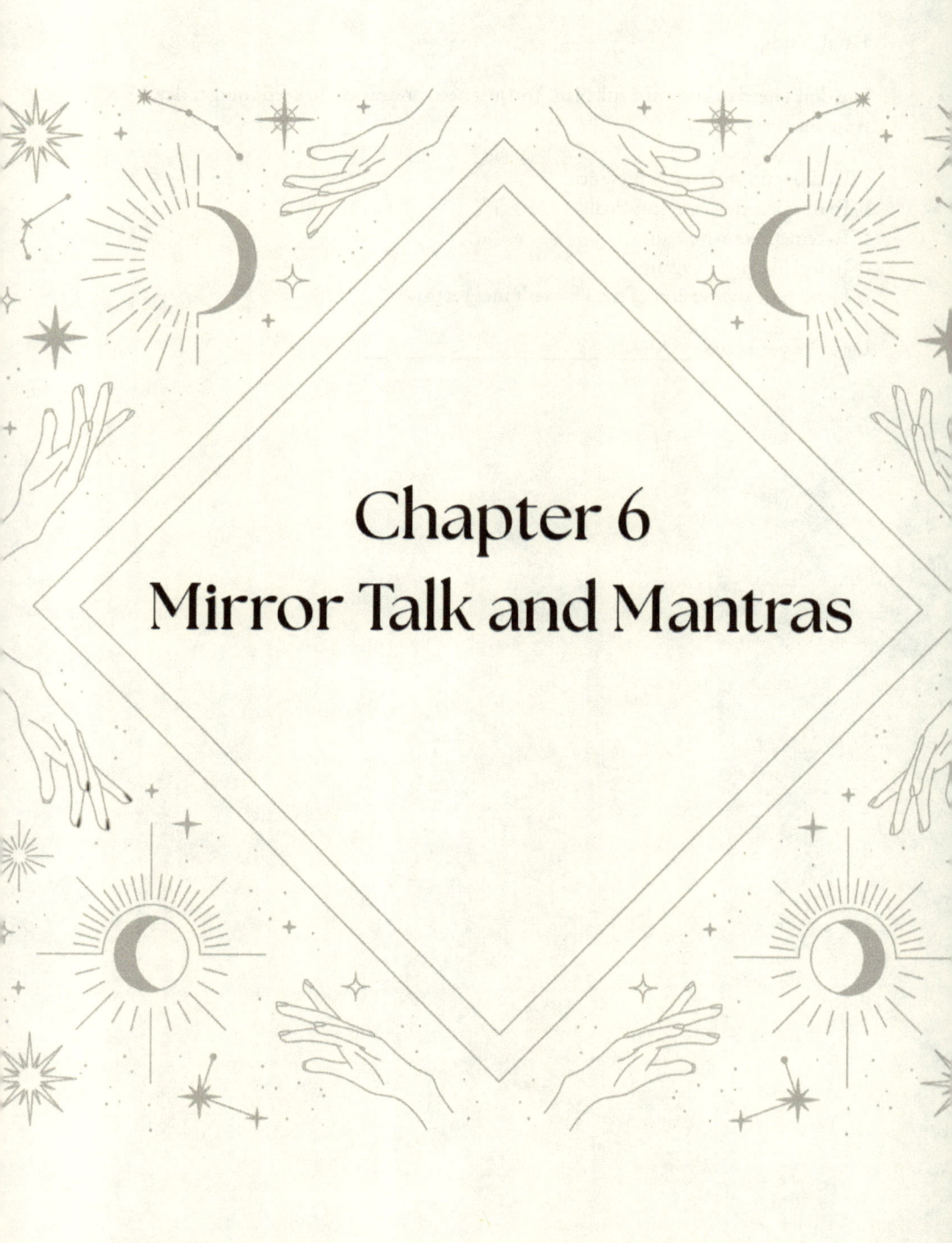

Chapter 6
Mirror Talk and Mantras

MIRROR TALK AND MANTRAS

Sometimes the fight isn't about taking action...it's about finding your voice, especially in the moments no one else hears. It's about what you say to yourself in the mirror after you've cried, broken down, or been overlooked. And for many of us, those words have been cruel for far too long.

Affirmations can feel fake in the beginning...like painting glitter over a cracked foundation. You might scoff. You might roll your eyes. You might feel ridiculous. But sometimes, wanting to believe them is enough to start. The work begins in stolen moments (before bed, after a breakdown, brushing your teeth) when you choose to interrupt the inner critic and speak something softer.

Mantras are more than "positive thinking." They're interruptions and invitations. Tiny acts of rebellion against the beliefs you've inherited, the shame you've carried, and the patterns that have kept you small. Each repetition presses a new path into the grass...awkward and uneven at first, but over time, it becomes a trail you can trust.

This isn't just for you. It's for the people who see you, love you, and learn from you. Every time you choose kindness instead of criticism, you not only rewire your own patterns, you model a different way of being. You give others permission to stay in the picture, to take up space, to see themselves as enough.

So say it again. Say it anyway. Even when it feels like a lie. Even when it's through tears. Even when it makes your skin crawl. You're teaching your nervous system what safety sounds like. You're staying in the frame. You're leaving a legacy that isn't built on shame.

Write one mantra on a sticky note, put it on your mirror, and say it out loud every day for the next 7 days, no matter how it feels in the moment. (Write as many as you can. I'll help you, too!)

_____
_____
_____
_____
_____
_____
_____
_____
_____
_____
_____
_____
_____
_____
_____

I am beautiful, I am worthy, I am enough. (Bet you didn't see that one coming! lol!)
I am allowed to be both a masterpiece and a work in progress.
I am allowed to rest.
My worth isn't something I prove. It's something I own.
I am safe to be seen, even if no one claps for me.
I do not have to shrink to be loved.
I remember who I am, even when others don't.
We don't do that anymore.

_____

Imagine a world where you're no longer here. What do your loved ones have to remember you by? How does that shift the way you see yourself in the present moment?

_____
_____
_____
_____
_____

_____
_____
_____
_____
_____
_____
_____
_____
_____
_____
_____

Write down three of your most common critical thoughts. For each one, create a mantra that directly interrupts it.

1.

2.

3.

Think of someone you love deeply. Write three mantras you wish they believed about themselves. Then—say them to yourself.

_____
_____
_____
_____
_____
_____
_____
_____
_____
_____
_____
_____
_____
_____
_____

What's one mantra you've heard that stuck with you, even if you didn't believe it at the time?_____
_____

_____

_____

_____

_____

_____

_____

_____

_____

_____

_____

_____

_____

_____

Reflect on the voices from your childhood. Which phrases about worth or appearance do you still carry? Which ones need rewriting?

_____

_____

_____

_____

_____

_____

_____

_____

_____

_____

_____

_____

_____

_____

Describe what it feels like in your body when you say something kind to yourself and actually believe it.

_____

_____

_____

_____

_____

_____

_____
_____
_____
_____
_____
_____
_____
_____
_____
_____

What would change if your child, partner, or best friend spoke to themselves the way you speak to yourself?

_____
_____
_____
_____
_____
_____
_____
_____
_____
_____
_____
_____
_____
_____

Write a mantra specifically for the days when the noise in your head gets louder instead of quieter.

_____
_____
_____
_____
_____
_____
_____
_____
_____
_____

_____

_____

_____

_____

_____

Your mantras are not a performance. They are a private revolution. Every time you speak one, you bend the grass on a new path toward the version of you who believes she's enough. At first, you're just visiting that version. Eventually, she's home. Keep speaking. Keep interrupting. Keep staying in the picture.

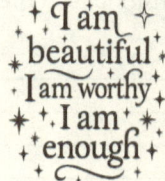

Chapter 7
Mindfulness

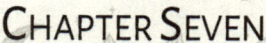

CHAPTER SEVEN

MINDFULNESS

M indfulness isn't always calm. It's clarity, and clarity can hurt. Stillness brings up the chaos you've been avoiding, and once you hear it, you can't un-hear it. That's why you need filters (your "velvet rope") to decide what gets in and what stays out. Protecting your peace isn't cold. It's how you stay present for yourself and the people you love.

What came up for you while reading this chapter?
(Ex: emotions, memories, patterns, thoughts that felt too loud)

→

→

→

Now pause. Choose one of those and finish this sentence:
This came up because I'm learning to...

What thoughts have I let in recently that don't belong to me?
_____
_____
_____
_____
_____
_____
_____
_____
_____
_____
_____
_____
_____
_____
_____
_____
_____
_____
_____
_____
_____
_____
_____
_____
_____
_____
_____
_____
_____
_____
_____

Which filter do I need to strengthen right now?

_____
_____
_____
_____
_____
_____
_____
_____
_____
_____
_____
_____
_____
_____
_____
_____

What energy am I allowing that feels like spam?

_____
_____
_____
_____
_____
_____
_____
_____
_____
_____
_____
_____
_____
_____
_____
_____

Is there something I've outgrown but still allow in out of habit?

_____
_____
_____
_____
_____

_____
_____
_____
_____
_____
_____
_____
_____
_____
_____
_____

If my peace had a velvet rope, what would I stop letting in today?

_____
_____
_____
_____
_____
_____
_____
_____
_____
_____
_____
_____
_____
_____

The Filter Audit – List three recent moments that left you feeling drained. For each, ask: Was this about me or them? What filter could I have used?

_____
_____
_____
_____
_____
_____
_____

_____

_____

_____

_____

_____

_____

_____

Energy Check-In – Before entering a conversation, room, or social media scroll, ask yourself: *How am I feeling right now?* Then check again afterward. Notice the difference.

_____

_____

_____

_____

_____

_____

_____

_____

_____

_____

_____

_____

_____

_____

The Spam Folder – Write down five recurring thoughts or comments that don't serve you. Move them to your "mental spam folder" and decide what to feed your mind instead.

_____

_____

_____

_____

_____

_____

_____

_____

_____

_____

_____

_____
_____
_____
_____
_____

Mindfulness in Motion – Identify an activity (like running, dancing, cooking, or talking with a trusted friend) that forces you into the present moment without trying. Describe how it shifts your energy.

_____
_____
_____
_____
_____
_____
_____
_____
_____
_____
_____
_____
_____
_____

The Conversation I'm Avoiding – Name one truth you've been swallowing. What would change if you said it out loud?

_____
_____
_____
_____
_____
_____
_____
_____
_____
_____
_____

_____
_____
_____

The Velvet Rope List – Who or what gets a front-row seat in your life right now? Who stays outside for now? Who gets "call back later" access?

_____
_____
_____
_____
_____
_____
_____
_____
_____
_____
_____
_____
_____
_____
_____

Body Listening – Try the 30-second reset: hand on chest, inhale 4, hold 4, exhale 6. Name one emotion. Describe where you feel it in your body.

_____
_____
_____
_____
_____
_____
_____
_____

_____
_____
_____
_____
_____
_____

Stillness isn't the absence of noise...it's the awareness of what's worth hearing. Filters keep your mind clear and your energy yours, so when the world gets loud, you still know your own voice.

reclaiming joy

```
                          X
                        Q I G
                      Y Q Z C K
                    E E R F Q Z D
                  C R C Z C E P T J
                A F L O W E J K E O K
              E G I R C L W W F I N K G
            P R B L I S S P Z D V L V J M
          A Y N K Y G T A L I V E N D W V C
        I S F E R K A G B Q K R T O Q L Z P R
      W H U Q A A V M I G C E F A I H O I F B T
    L X N T K I D K E P F T L N D T H M J H L G W
  A Q D D E U Z I G X G H W U Z X A W E A Z C P H P
  C P M L J Z Y N A K N G T O G Z A R M C W V R Q J E K
G D F G K S P A J N Q U V Z Q L B Y B O F W L K B U V E K
Y H I H Q W P Z X A T A X C M P T U F E K C W X P T V V S Y N
M S U F V N A D S H I L B S Q D K W R V L O I P F W A L M O T J Q
D I U M H L H Q I W L G X B P O R H L P I E T Q J O S V D X N C Y C Q
V R K J A I D S P I Q Z L L D N I D E R K X C U O J X I B S I G M Z D V P
Y I J B D J P L W Y O B D A K L Y S T G R Y F V P W A K L Q I K A A B W T K F
X H W F W T U E N A S W T Z O D A N C E M P U A P I O H X Z D O B A S D K
G G D S A N H F C X N S H P D K D Z S H V I K L E M Y P A V W C Z O D
L J S J Y E E H S C O X O B U A F P I S K W J M C Q W M U S I C Y
J M X E D M Q P A N H L I G H T K G K L R E V T O M F F I Q V
F H Q N U E N N Y C P T F Z Z V Z M L X B B X G A X A D O
A B B Z T V L D N O B N R N Y S J Q Z E E W U E G Y A
V R P N N O I V M W V L F I M N K Z R B T Q A C X
R G N N F M U U I D O L F Q D A N J I G V U W
E Z G T I C V R H L G T B O C B A C V G C
Z M Y F R K B Y U B H U O H A F F K U
E J Y L A R R V A E L U Q J K Y B
X T J V G A L X O B L Z Y Q Z
U L R N I P R G Z M J D O
E R Q O P S L T A E I
I Q V L D K Y S U
V E A L K B I
J Y M Z N
L T Q
N
```

WORD LIST

ALIVE	FLOW	MOVEMENT	SILLY
BLISS	FUN	MUSIC	SMILE
CELEBRATION	GAME	NOSTALGIA	SONG
CHILDLIKE	HAPPY	PEACE	SPARK
COLOR	LAUGHTER	PLAY	
DANCE	LIGHT	RADIANT	

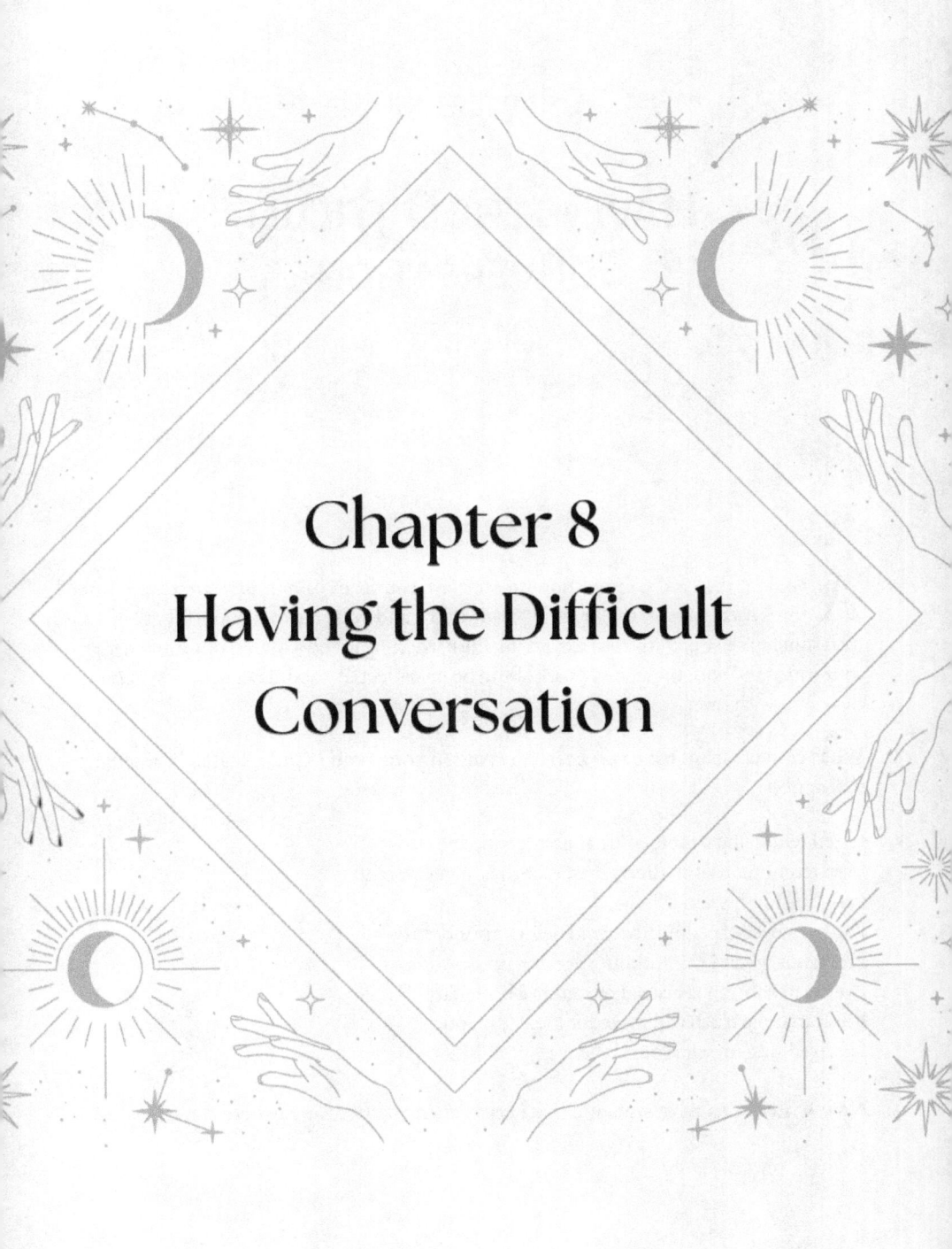

Chapter 8
Having the Difficult Conversation

HAVING THE DIFFICULT CONVERSATION

A voiding the hard conversation doesn't save you from pain; it just stretches it out until it eats away at your peace, your body, and your relationships. Whether it's with someone else or with yourself, saying the hard thing is how you reclaim your energy, your truth, and your presence. It's not about being perfect. It's about being honest...clean, clear, and with love.

What conversation have you been carrying in your body? Circle/highlight anything that applies:

I keep rehearsing a moment that hasn't happened
I feel resentment or tension when I see their name pop up
I say "it's fine" when it's not
I've been over-explaining to avoid being misunderstood
I feel guilt when I think about speaking up
I've created distance instead of setting a boundary
I'm scared the truth will make me look "too much"
I keep editing myself around them

Now, write the name or situation that keeps coming up (we'll dig in here in a sec):

The conversation I've been avoiding is with: _____

The truth I've been swallowing is: _____

What difficult conversation have I been avoiding?

_____

_____

_____

_____

_____

_____

_____

_____

_____

_____

_____

_____

_____

_____

_____

What truth have I been swallowing to keep the peace?

_____

_____

_____

_____

_____

_____

_____

_____

_____

_____

_____

_____

_____

_____

_____

What do I want from this conversation—clarity, closure, boundaries, reconnection?

_____
_____
_____
_____
_____
_____
_____
_____
_____
_____
_____
_____
_____
_____
_____

What am I afraid will happen if I speak up?

_____
_____
_____
_____
_____
_____
_____
_____
_____
_____
_____
_____
_____
_____

What might finally happen if I do?

_____
_____
_____
_____
_____

_____
_____
_____
_____
_____
_____
_____
_____
_____
_____
_____
_____

Before / During / After – Visualize yourself having the conversation. What sensations come up in your body before, during, and after?

_____
_____
_____
_____
_____
_____
_____
_____
_____
_____
_____
_____
_____
_____
_____

Fear vs. Freedom – Write down your biggest fear about speaking your truth, and then list three freedoms you might gain from saying it anyway.

_____
_____
_____
_____
_____
_____
_____

_____

_____

_____

_____

_____

_____

_____

_____

The Self-Conversation – Identify an area where _you_ have been crossing your own boundaries. Write a letter to yourself as if you were your own best friend.

_____

_____

_____

_____

_____

_____

_____

_____

_____

_____

_____

_____

_____

_____

Micro-Moments of Honesty – What are three small truths you can practice saying this week to build confidence for the bigger ones?

_____

_____

_____

_____

_____

_____

_____

_____

_____
_____
_____
_____
_____
_____

When Love Says No – Reflect on one situation where saying no (to yourself or someone else) was an act of love. How did it feel in the long run?

_____
_____
_____
_____
_____
_____
_____
_____
_____
_____
_____
_____
_____
_____

The 30-Day Integrity Check – For the next month, notice every time you say "It's fine" when it isn't. Track what those moments are costing you.

_____
_____
_____
_____
_____
_____
_____
_____
_____
_____

_____
_____
_____

Conversation Gains List – Create your personal "Why It's Worth It" list. Keep it visible for the moments you want to back down.

_____
_____
_____
_____
_____
_____
_____
_____
_____
_____
_____
_____
_____
_____
_____
_____

Cost vs. Gain: The Conversation Truth Table

Fill this in based on your *specific* situation.

If I Keep Avoiding This...
Example: I lose sleep replaying it.

If I Finally Say the Damn Thing...
I get peace, even if it's messy.

Choose one that speaks to you (or write your own).

- "I can be kind and clear at the same time."

- "My truth doesn't need approval to be valid."

- "Silence isn't safety...it's slow self-abandonment."

- "Peace isn't found in pretending."

- "I'm not breaking anything by being honest. I'm unbreaking myself."

    Write your own: _____

One Last Thing...

Who do I want to be on the other side of this conversation?
Not how they respond. Not what changes. Just *you*. Hold that version close.

After this, I will walk more like...☐

_____

_____

_____

_____

_____

_____

_____

_____

_____

_____

_____

_____

_____

_____

_____

The conversation might not fix the relationship, the dynamic, or the outcome...but it will set you free. Honesty is an act of courage, and courage is how you come back to yourself. Speak the truth, hold your boundaries, and remember: peace isn't always soft. Sometimes it's raw. Sometimes it hurts. And sometimes, it's the only way back home.

YOUR ORACLE PULL

Pick a number that calls to you.
Flip to the back to reveal your message.

Chapter 9
Show and Tell

SHOW AND TELL

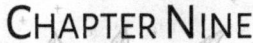

Healing doesn't end when you find the words...it begins when you live them. Chapter 9 calls you to close the gap between what you say you believe and how you actually show up in your life. This isn't about performative growth or perfectly packaged vulnerability; it's about letting your daily choices reflect your values, even when it's messy, quiet, or unseen. It's the adult version of "show and tell," where instead of holding up a toy, you hold up your truth. You stop performing confidence and start building self-trust through action...one aligned choice at a time.

Where am I still performing healing instead of practicing it?

_____
_____
_____
_____
_____
_____
_____
_____
_____
_____
_____
_____
_____
_____
_____
_____
_____
_____

_____

_____

What truth have I been speaking, but not living?*(Example: "I need rest" but I never slow down. "I love myself" but I talk to my body like it's an enemy.)*

_____

_____

_____

_____

_____

_____

_____

_____

_____

_____

_____

_____

_____

_____

_____

What's one small thing I could do this week to show the healing I've been telling myself I'm doing?

_____

_____

_____

_____

_____

_____

_____

_____

_____

_____

_____

_____

_____

_____

_____

If someone watched me for a full day but couldn't hear me speak, what would they say I believe about myself?

_____
_____
_____
_____
_____
_____
_____
_____
_____
_____
_____
_____
_____
_____
_____
_____

Now flip it: What do I *want* my actions to say about me?

_____
_____
_____
_____
_____
_____
_____
_____
_____
_____
_____
_____
_____
_____

Think about a time you *almost* acted in alignment but pulled back. What stopped you? What would you do differently next time?

_____

_____

_____

_____

_____

_____

_____

_____

_____

_____

_____

_____

_____

_____

_____

_____

_____

Write about one value you deeply believe in. How can you show it (not just say it) this week?

_____

_____

_____

_____

_____

_____

_____

_____

_____

_____

_____

_____

_____

_____

_____
_____

Make a list of five "micro-actions" that would move you toward alignment in your daily life. Circle one to commit to for the next 7 days.

1.

2.

3.

4.

5.

Describe a moment you've witnessed someone else living their truth unapologetically. What about it inspired you?

_____
_____
_____
_____
_____
_____

_____
_____
_____
_____
_____
_____
_____
_____
_____
_____
_____
_____

What is one action you could take today that your future self will thank you for?

_____
_____
_____
_____
_____
_____
_____
_____
_____
_____
_____
_____
_____
_____
_____
_____
_____

Where in your life are you waiting for confidence before taking action? How could you reverse it and let action *create* confidence?

_____
_____
_____
_____
_____
_____
_____

_____
_____
_____
_____
_____
_____
_____
_____
_____
_____
_____

If your healing journey were a show-and-tell object, what would it be and why? Write about it in detail.

_____
_____
_____
_____
_____
_____
_____
_____
_____
_____
_____
_____
_____
_____
_____
_____
_____
_____

You've said the thing. You've written it, whispered it, prayed it, posted it. Now it's time to walk it. Because the world doesn't just need to hear your truth...it needs to feel it through the way you live. Not perfectly. Not performatively. Just honestly. And if you're still shaky? That's okay. Show up anyway. Because your life isn't just the story you tell...it's the proof you leave behind.

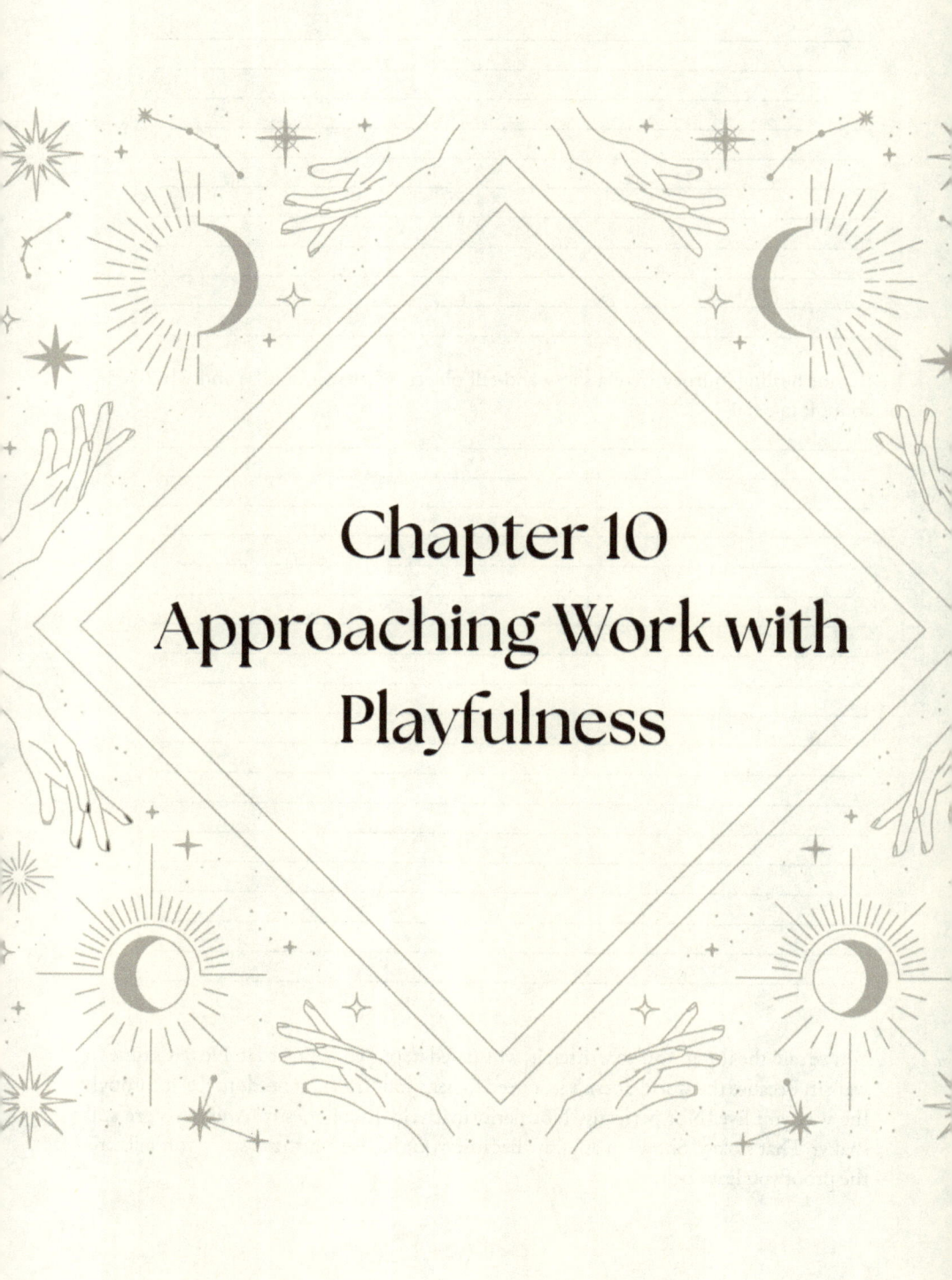

Chapter 10
Approaching Work with Playfulness

APPROACHING WORK WITH PLAYFULNESS

W ork doesn't have to be heavy to be meaningful. We've been conditioned to believe play is childish and productivity only counts if it drains us, but the truth is, play is fuel. It's where creativity comes alive, where our nervous system exhales, and where alignment feels magnetic. Play isn't chaos; it's aliveness. It's not about forcing joy, it's about finding it. When you follow curiosity instead of perfection, you create space for ease, freedom, and the kind of work that actually lights you up.

Where have I made work too serious?

_____
_____
_____
_____
_____
_____
_____
_____
_____
_____
_____
_____
_____
_____
_____
_____
_____
_____

_____

_____

What would it look like to bring more play into my process?

_____

_____

_____

_____

_____

_____

_____

_____

_____

_____

_____

_____

_____

_____

_____

What did I love to do as a kid that I've abandoned?

_____

_____

_____

_____

_____

_____

_____

_____

_____

_____

_____

_____

_____

_____

_____

What if I didn't need to "earn" rest, joy, or laughter?

_____
_____
_____
_____
_____
_____
_____
_____
_____
_____
_____
_____
_____
_____
_____
_____
_____
_____

Where am I using "I'll be happy when..." logic in my life or work?

_____
_____
_____
_____
_____

_____

_____

_____

_____

_____

_____

_____

_____

_____

_____

_____

_____

What would change if I brought joy into the process instead of waiting for the outcome?

_____

_____

_____

_____

_____

_____

_____

_____

_____

_____

_____

_____

_____

_____

_____

What does "play" feel like in my body, how do I recognize it?

_____

_____

_____

_____

_____

_____

_____
_____
_____
_____
_____
_____
_____
_____
_____
_____

Where am I confusing play with procrastination or laziness?

_____
_____
_____
_____
_____
_____
_____
_____
_____
_____
_____
_____
_____

How can I create a playful ritual in my workday this week?

_____
_____
_____
_____
_____
_____
_____

_____
_____
_____
_____
_____
_____
_____
_____

What's one area of my life that feels rigid, how could I loosen it with curiosity?

_____
_____
_____
_____
_____
_____
_____
_____
_____
_____
_____
_____
_____
_____

When was the last time I laughed while working on something? How can I invite that in again?

_____
_____
_____
_____
_____
_____
_____
_____
_____
_____

What's one tiny, weird, or "pointless" thing that would make today lighter?

Reclaim Your Inner Kid: What did 7-year-old you LOVE to do? No wrong answers. Crayons, puddles, collecting shiny rocks...it all counts.

Things I loved as a kid:

☐

☐

☐

Now ask:
Where have I abandoned that version of me?

How can I bring her back into my grown-up world?

Even just one way. Try it.

Unhook from the Hustle: Complete these prompts honestly:

☐   I've believed success means:
→ _____

☐   I used to think joy had to be:
→ _____

☐   But now I'm realizing:
→ _____

Flip the Script: Choose a project or goal you're working on and write it below. Then reframe it like a game, an experiment, or a dare.

Current Goal or Project:
→ _____

Now reframe it:
→ *"What if I approached this like..."*
A treasure hunt
A science experiment
A messy art project
A dance
Something no one ever has to see

Write your playful version here:
→

Play isn't something you wait for...it's something you choose. Every time you let yourself laugh, shift, experiment, or follow curiosity, you're rewriting what success feels like in your body. You don't have to hustle your way into alignment; you can play your way into it. And the more you let joy into the process, the more magnetic your work (and your life) become.

Chapter 11
Removing the Judgey Adult

REMOVING THE JUDGEY ADULT

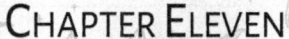

The Judgey Adult isn't your Ego, but she's her cousin. Where Ego keeps you hidden in fear of failure, the Judgey Adult lets you be seen, just edited, polished, and palatable. Her weapon isn't doubt, it's judgment. She's the "what will people think?" voice, the inner critic who insists on beige. She thrives when you grow, because joy, rest, and play are chaos to her...uncontrollable, unmeasurable, unapproved. But her voice is not truth. She was created by systems and survival, not your soul. You don't need her permission to expand. You only need your own.

What does your inner Judgey Adult say the most?

_____

_____

_____

_____

_____

_____

_____

_____

_____

_____

_____

_____

_____

_____

Whose voice does it sound like?

_____

_____
_____
_____
_____
_____
_____
_____
_____
_____
_____
_____
_____

What's something you've wanted to do, but haven't because you were afraid of being judged?

_____
_____
_____
_____
_____
_____
_____
_____
_____
_____
_____
_____
_____

What are you fighting for?

_____
_____
_____
_____
_____
_____
_____
_____
_____

_____
_____
_____
_____

What do you gain if you do it anyway?

_____
_____
_____
_____
_____
_____
_____
_____
_____
_____
_____
_____

What do you lose if you keep shrinking to keep her comfortable?

_____
_____
_____
_____
_____
_____
_____
_____
_____
_____
_____
_____
_____

What specific moments in your past can you remember when judgment shut you down? Write them down...then underline the ones that still influence you today.

_____
_____
_____

_____

_____

_____

_____

_____

_____

_____

_____

_____

_____

If your Judgey Adult had a uniform, what would she be wearing? (Make her ridiculous if you need to...it helps loosen her grip.)

_____

_____

_____

_____

_____

_____

_____

_____

_____

_____

_____

_____

What triggers her most? Your joy, your rest, your creativity, or your boldness? Doodle your answers here, then circle it.

How does your body feel when she's loud? How does your body feel when you ignore her?

_____
_____
_____
_____
_____
_____
_____
_____
_____
_____
_____
_____
_____
_____

Write a "thank you" letter to your Judgey Adult: thank her for trying to keep you safe, acknowledge how she's different than your Ego, then dismiss her from the job.

_____
_____
_____
_____
_____
_____
_____
_____
_____
_____
_____
_____
_____

Prove Her Wrong: Pick ONE thing you've been scared to do because of how it might look, sound, or come off to others—and **do it anyway** this week. Doesn't have to be huge. Just has to be _true._

My brave rebellion this week is:

Then write how it felt. Even if it was awkward. Even if the Judgey Adult screamed. Especially then.

The Permission Slip Rebellion ☐

Grab a scrap of paper (nothing fancy). At the top, write:

"Permission Slip"

Now, let your Judgey Adult rant. Write down her rules in her exact words — all the "shoulds," "too much's," and "not enough's." Don't filter. Let her nag. Get it all out.

Then — here's the twist. At the bottom of the page, you sign it. Not as the Judgey Adult. But as your **truest, messiest, most unapologetic self.** Write:

"I hereby give myself permission to break every single one of these rules."

Tear the slip in half. Pocket the bottom (the signed permission) and toss or burn the rest.

Now, every time you hear her voice creep back in, tap the slip in your pocket (or picture it in your mind if you've let it go) and remind yourself: *I already gave myself permission.*

Because the Judgey Adult thrives on authority — but the second you realize you're the authority now, her clipboard loses its power.

I'll add some space on this page too, just in case you'd prefer it here!

_____

_____

_____

_____

_____

_____

_____

_____

_____

_____

_____

_____

_____

_____

_____

_____

_____

_____

_____

_____

_____

_____

_____

_____

_____

_____

_____

_____

_____

_____

_____

_____

I _____ hereby give myself permission to break every single one of these rules. Date:_____

Your Judgey Adult will always try to keep you safe, but safety at the cost of your soul isn't safety — it's a cage. She'll call it "responsible." She'll call it "realistic." But you already know the truth: joy, play, rest, and expression are not luxuries, they're lifelines. Every time you laugh too loud, create something weird, or choose rest without permission, you loosen her grip. You don't have to silence her forever — just stop letting her steer. Because your worth was never in her spreadsheets.

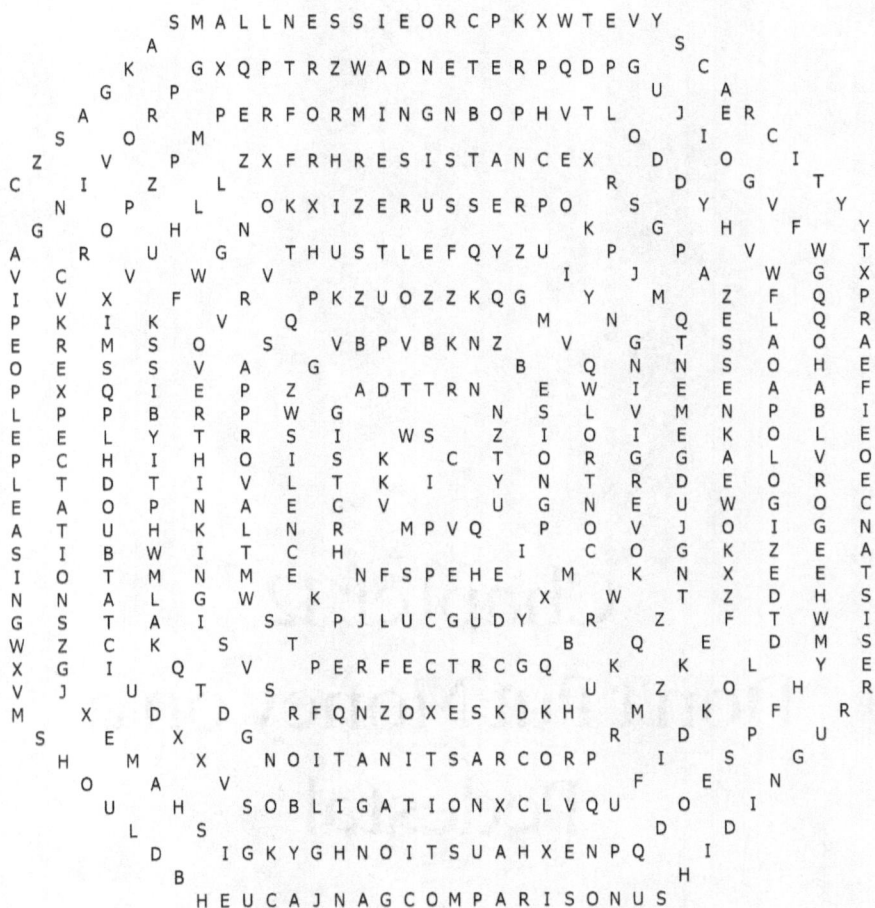

WORD LIST

APOLOGIZE	FEAR	PEOPLE PLEASING	RESISTANCE
APPROVAL	HIDING	PERFECT	SCARCITY
COMPARISON	HUSTLE	PERFORMING	SHAME
CONTROL	JUDGEMENT	PRESSURE	SHOULD
DOUBT	NOISE	PRETEND	SILENCE
GO	OBLIGATION	PROCRASTINATION	SMALLNESS
EXHAUSTION	OVERGIVING	PROVING	WEAKNESS
EXPECTATIONS	OVERTHINKING	RESISTANCE	

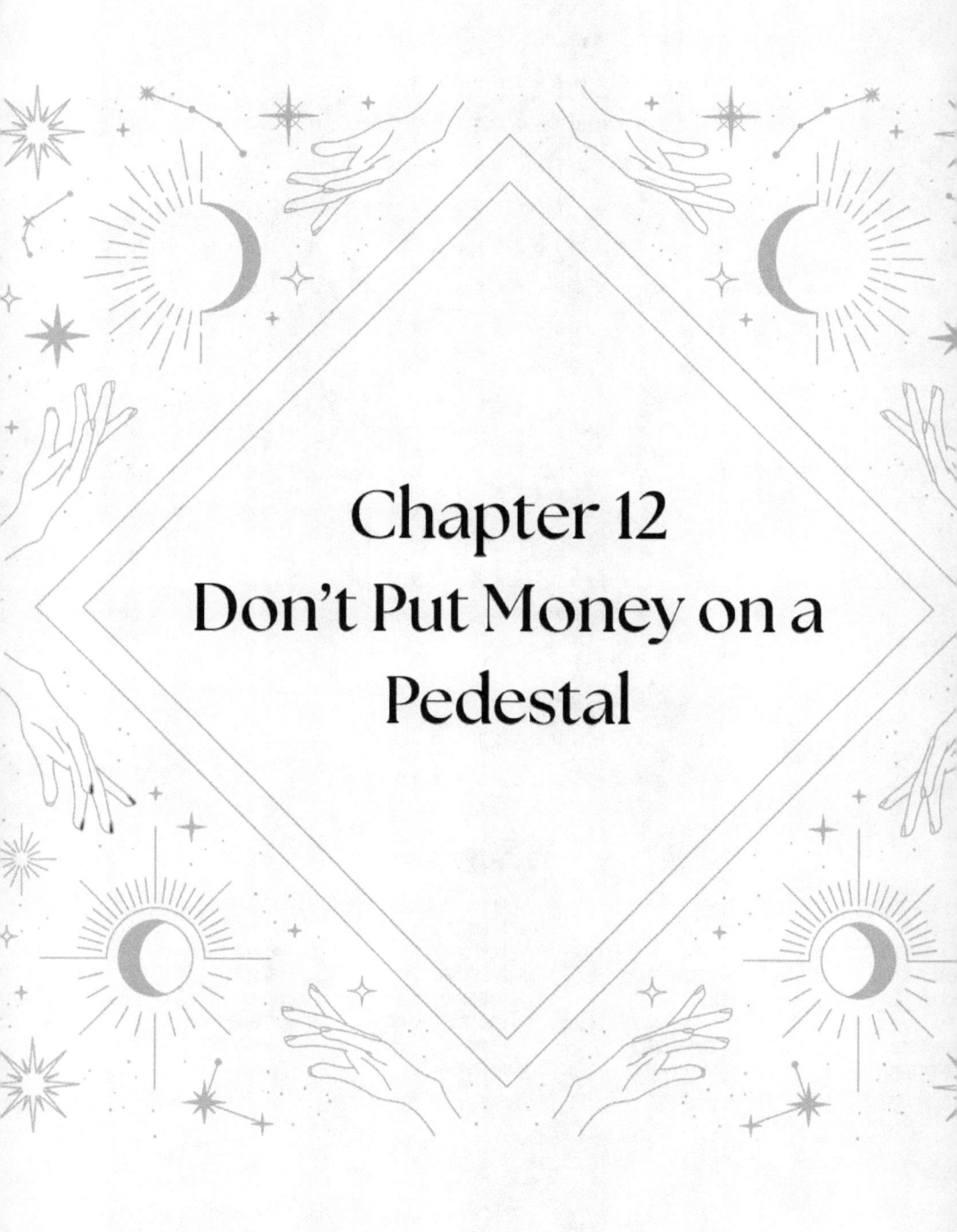

Chapter 12
Don't Put Money on a Pedestal

DON'T PUT MONEY ON A PEDESTAL

Money is not your proof, not your identity, not your worth. It's just a tool. When you put it on a pedestal, you betray yourself to chase it, but when you let values drive, money becomes a partner instead of a ruler. The Universe echoes your beliefs... so when you speak from desperation, you get more reasons to panic. When you speak from assurance, you start to notice relief, provision, and overflow. Your worth was never meant to be graded by your bank account. Alignment first, money second.

What story were you told about money growing up?

_____
_____
_____
_____
_____
_____
_____
_____
_____
_____
_____
_____
_____
_____
_____
_____

When have you compromised your values in pursuit of money?

_____
_____

_____
_____
_____
_____
_____
_____
_____
_____
_____
_____
_____

When have you chosen alignment over income, and how did it feel?

_____
_____
_____
_____
_____
_____
_____
_____
_____
_____
_____
_____

What does true success look like for you, outside of numbers?

_____
_____
_____
_____
_____
_____
_____
_____
_____
_____
_____

_____
_____
_____

Finish the sentence:

I don't want to suffer my success. I want to

_____
_____

I don't want the money to feel like power. I want it to feel like

_____
_____

Let's dig a little deeper...

Where do I still believe "more money = more worth"?

_____
_____
_____
_____
_____
_____
_____
_____
_____
_____
_____
_____
_____

What emotions come up when I look at my bank account? What do they reveal about my beliefs?

_____
_____
_____
_____
_____
_____
_____
_____
_____
_____
_____

_____
_____
_____

When has money amplified joy instead of stress? What's different about those moments?

_____
_____
_____
_____
_____
_____
_____
_____
_____
_____
_____

What would shift if I stopped pedestalizing money and started rehearsing peace instead?

_____
_____
_____
_____
_____
_____
_____
_____
_____
_____
_____
_____

How can I remind myself that "I'm supported" even when it feels scary?

_____
_____
_____
_____

_____
_____
_____
_____
_____
_____
_____
_____

What small, aligned action can I take this week that isn't driven by money but by values?

_____
_____
_____
_____
_____
_____
_____
_____
_____
_____
_____
_____

This next question is loaded, so I want to give you some more info before we jump into it. The question is: **What affirmations feel true enough for me to say out loud right now (not bypassing, but re-directing)?** But what does that mean exactly?

1. **"True enough"** – You don't need to jump all the way to "I'm a millionaire" when you're stressed about bills (your body won't believe it.)

Instead, you choose affirmations that feel believable right now. They stretch you, but they don't break trust with yourself.

Example:
"I have unlimited money, always." (feels fake when your account is low)
"We've been here before, and we made it through. We always do." (still true, still grounding)

2. **"Say out loud"** Words have power... when you actually speak them, you anchor the energy in your nervous system.

It shifts you from *thinking* differently to *embodying* it differently.

3. **"Not bypassing, but re-directing"** *Bypassing* is pretending the hard stuff isn't happening ("I'm not broke, everything is perfect!").

Re-directing is acknowledging the hard, but choosing a truer anchor.

Example:
If your brain says: *"There's never enough."*

Re-direct with: *"Money always flows in and out. Right now I'm in the in-between, and that's okay."*

So really, this question is an invitation to:

-Notice where affirmations feel too fake/performative.
-Choose words that feel *grounded and believable enough* that your body can relax into them.
-Practice shifting your language gently, without denying your reality.

So now, let's answer: What affirmations feel true enough for me to say out loud right now (not bypassing, but re-directing)?

_____
_____
_____
_____
_____
_____
_____
_____
_____

_____
_____
_____
_____
_____

Reframing
-Money is a tool, not a trophy.
-Money is a partner, not a parent.
-Money is a resource, not a ruler.
-Money doesn't get to grade your worth.

Which one of these reframes feels most needed for me right now? Why?

_____
_____
_____
_____
_____
_____
_____
_____
_____
_____
_____
_____
_____
_____

Journal This:

What was your earliest memory of money feeling either powerful or painful?
Describe the scene. Who was there? What did you feel in your body?

_____

_____

_____

_____

_____

_____

_____

_____

_____

_____

_____

_____

_____

_____

What messages did you absorb growing up about money and worth?
Think: "We don't talk about money," "Money doesn't grow on trees," "You have to work hard to earn your place," etc. Which ones still linger in your decision-making?

_____

_____

_____

_____

_____

_____

_____

_____

_____

_____

_____

_____

_____

What do you currently believe about people who have a lot of money? And people who don't?
Get honest. Notice what comes up (envy, resentment, admiration, judgment). Whose voice is behind those beliefs?

_____

_____

_____

_____
_____
_____
_____
_____
_____
_____
_____
_____
_____
_____

Where in your life have you said yes just because you were afraid to say no to money?
Circle or list examples where fear made the call instead of values.

_____
_____
_____
_____
_____
_____
_____
_____
_____
_____
_____
_____
_____
_____

Fill in the blanks with your truth.

I once chased money at the expense of _____.
I once felt safest when my bank account hit \$_____, but what I really needed was
_____.
I used to believe money = _____, but now I know it's just _____.
I betrayed myself when I said yes to _____, even though _____.
I've made aligned choices even when they scared me, like _____. That moment
taught me _____.

What *actually* makes you feel rich (hint: it's probably not just the numbers)?

_____
_____

_____
_____
_____
_____
_____
_____
_____
_____
_____
_____
_____
_____
_____

Money is never the mirror of your worth. It's just the echo of what you're rehearsing. Lead with your values. Choose assurance over desperation. And remember: the Universe is listening to the words you speak...so let it overhear your *faith*, not your *fear*.

Doodle Break. Make a page of doodle confetti... circles, stars, hearts, squiggles, waves, trees, spirals, words (enough, breathe, peace, worthy, beautiful, silly) — and let it spill everywhere.

Chapter 13
Happy Money

HAPPY MONEY

M oney carries the energy you give it. Spend in fear, and it shrinks. Spend in gratitude, and it grows. "Happy Money" isn't about having more... it's about shifting
how you relate to what you already have. When money feels like flow, trust, gratitude,
and joy, it multiplies. When it's loaded with fear, shame, or resentment, it depletes you.
Happy Money is intentional, grateful, and aligned. It reminds you that every dollar is part
of the life you're building, not a verdict on your worth.

How do you feel before, during, and after spending money?

_____
_____
_____
_____
_____
_____
_____
_____
_____
_____
_____
_____
_____
_____
_____

Do you tense up at checkout?

_____
_____

_____
_____
_____
_____
_____
_____
_____
_____
_____
_____
_____
_____
_____

Do you feel guilt after purchases, even necessary ones?

_____
_____
_____
_____
_____
_____
_____
_____
_____
_____
_____
_____

Can you spot the difference between anxious spending and intentional investing?

_____
_____
_____
_____
_____
_____
_____
_____
_____
_____
_____

_____
_____

What is my current relationship with money trying to teach me?

_____
_____
_____
_____
_____
_____
_____
_____
_____
_____
_____
_____
_____

Where am I spending from fear instead of flow?

_____
_____
_____
_____
_____
_____
_____
_____
_____
_____
_____
_____
_____
_____
_____

How would it feel to spend money with gratitude, no matter the amount?

_____
_____
_____
_____
_____
_____
_____
_____
_____
_____
_____
_____
_____
_____
_____

What emotions do I attach to bills, and how could I reframe them into gratitude?

_____
_____
_____
_____
_____
_____
_____
_____
_____
_____
_____
_____
_____
_____

Where in my life am I rehearsing "just enough," and what would "more than enough" look like?

_____
_____
_____
_____
_____

_____
_____
_____
_____
_____
_____
_____
_____

When was the last time I spent money in a way that felt joyful instead of stressful?

_____
_____
_____
_____
_____
_____
_____
_____
_____
_____
_____
_____
_____

What small ritual could I add when paying bills to shift the energy (e.g., saying "thank you" or writing a note of gratitude)?

_____
_____
_____
_____
_____
_____
_____
_____
_____
_____
_____
_____
_____

How do I model money energy for my kids, family, or community?

_____
_____
_____
_____
_____
_____
_____
_____
_____
_____
_____
_____
_____

What would it look like to make joy a line item in my budget?

_____
_____
_____
_____
_____
_____
_____
_____
_____
_____
_____
_____
_____

If I treated money as a partner instead of a problem, how would my decisions change?

_____
_____
_____
_____
_____
_____
_____
_____

_____
_____
_____
_____
_____

Where am I still holding onto shame around money, and how can I release it?
_____
_____
_____
_____
_____
_____
_____
_____
_____
_____
_____
_____
_____
_____
_____

What would it feel like if money trusted me as much as I wanted to trust it?
_____
_____
_____
_____
_____
_____
_____
_____
_____
_____
_____
_____
_____
_____

Energy Check-In: Money Moments Use this space to *honestly* reflect on how money feels in different situations. No shame. Just truth.

Situation	What I Usually Feel	What I Want to Feel Instead
Paying a bill		
Grocery shopping		
Spending on myself		
Investing in something joyful		
Receiving an unexpected fee or bill		
Talking about money with my family		

Money Mantras (Circle 3 to practice this week)
"Thanks, Universe. More please."
"Every dollar I spend returns to me doubled."
"Money supports the life I'm building."
"Spending is a sacred exchange."
"There's always more where that came from."
"I am grateful for what money makes possible."
"My money reflects my values."
"I spend with trust. I receive with joy."

Spend With Intention: Fill this out the next time you make a purchase—big or small.

Purchase

What it was for

Did I spend from fear or alignment?

Emotion after buying?

New Happy Money Thought

Happy Money isn't about chasing more...it's about honoring what's already in your hands. Every dollar can carry fear, or it can carry joy. Choose gratitude. Choose alignment. Because when money feels safe, intentional, and alive, it doesn't just pay the bills; it amplifies the life you're creating.

YOUR ORACLE
PULL

Pick a number that calls to you.
Flip to the back to reveal your message.

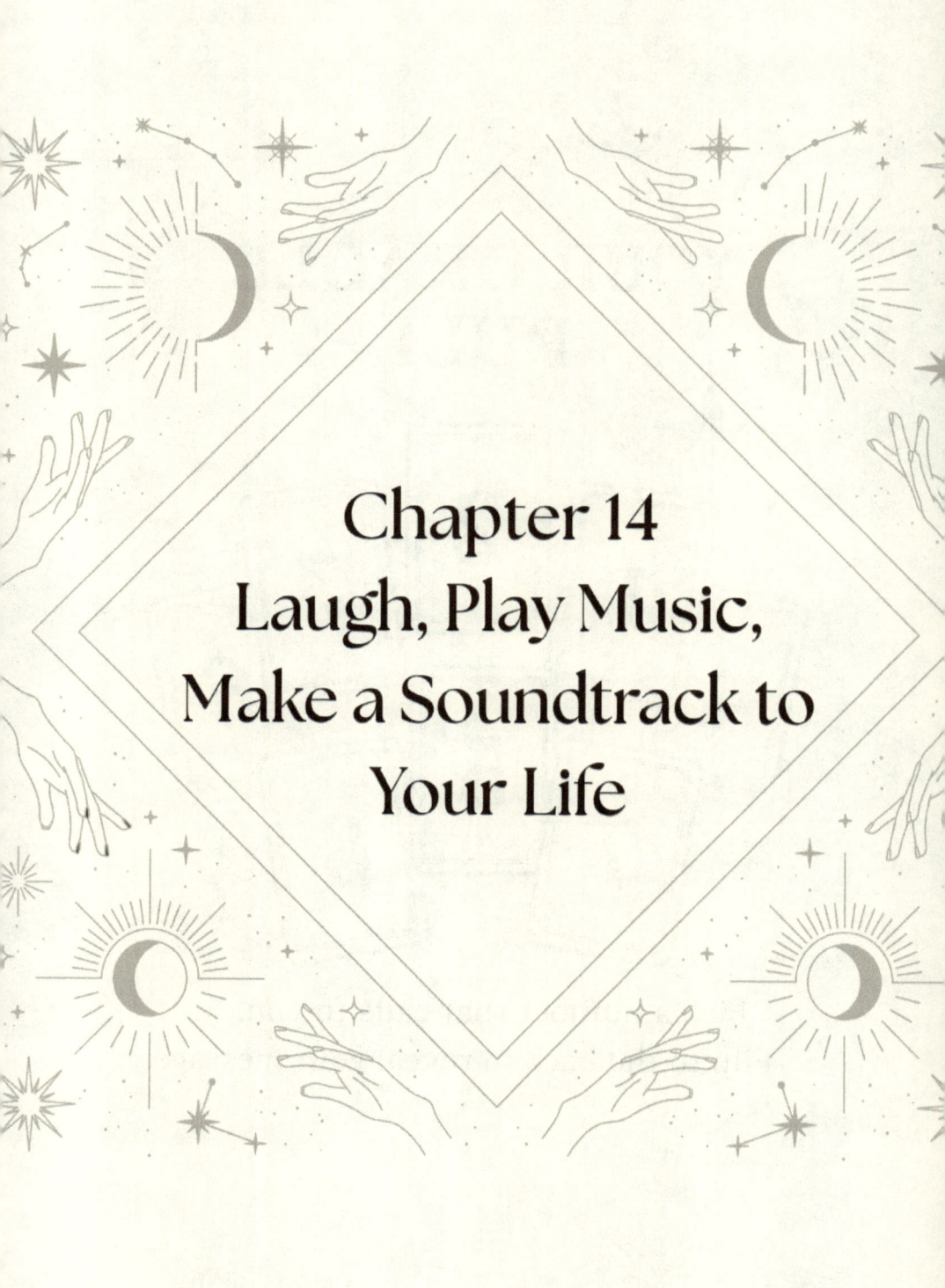

Chapter 14
Laugh, Play Music, Make a Soundtrack to Your Life

LAUGH, PLAY MUSIC, MAKE A SOUNDTRACK TO YOUR LIFE

J oy isn't an accident, it's a choice. Music is one of the fastest ways to remember that. Every season of your life has a soundtrack, whether you've been paying attention or not. Music pulls you back to yourself, lifts heaviness, creates connection, and anchors you in joy. Healing without joy isn't healing. Stop waiting for calm to feel alive. Press play now.

What song(s) makes you feel powerful? (like walk-through-fire, no-one-can-stop-me energy)

_____
_____
_____
_____
_____
_____
_____
_____
_____
_____
_____
_____
_____
_____

What song(s) makes you feel soft? Safe? Nostalgic?

_____

_____
_____
_____
_____
_____
_____
_____
_____
_____
_____
_____
_____
_____

What's a song that instantly makes you laugh or move your body? (For me, the ones that make me laugh are tied to memories, jot down the memory that comes up, too.)

_____
_____
_____
_____
_____
_____
_____
_____
_____
_____
_____
_____
_____

What was the soundtrack to one of the hardest seasons of your life?

_____
_____
_____
_____
_____
_____
_____

_____
_____
_____
_____
_____

What's a song that helped you heal, even if you didn't realize it at the time?

_____
_____
_____
_____
_____
_____
_____
_____
_____
_____
_____
_____
_____

Fill in the Blank

When I hear _____, I feel unstoppable.

The song that always makes me smile is _____.

If my life right now had an opening credits song, it would be
_____.

Circle One
What's the current *soundtrack* of your life?
☐ Loud & chaotic
☐ Quiet & numb
☐ Soft & steady
☐ Joyful & playful
☐ Healing & hopeful

Check Boxes
Which ways do you most often let music move you?
☐ Singing in the car
☐ Dancing in the kitchen
☐ Crying to a song that "gets it"

☐ Blasting a playlist while cleaning
☐ Sharing songs with friends/family
☐ Putting on headphones to reset my energy

Doodle Prompt
Draw a simple shape, symbol, or line that represents what joy feels like in your body when music is playing. Don't overthink it.

Which playlists hold the "eras" of your life, and what do they remind you of?

_____
_____
_____
_____
_____

_____
_____
_____
_____
_____
_____
_____
_____
_____
_____

Who have you connected with through music, and what did it open up between you?

_____
_____
_____
_____
_____
_____
_____
_____
_____
_____
_____
_____

What would it look like to create a "healing soundtrack", a playlist that meets you in the chaos but reminds you to laugh, breathe, and feel alive again?

_____
_____
_____
_____
_____
_____
_____
_____
_____
_____
_____
_____

How can I bring music in more intentionally, not just as background, but as guidance?

_____
_____
_____
_____
_____
_____
_____
_____
_____
_____
_____
_____
_____

What would the playlist of your **teenage years** sound like? When was the last time you heard some of that music? Next time you're in your car, I challenge you to listen to that era.

_____
_____
_____
_____
_____
_____
_____
_____
_____
_____
_____
_____
_____

What song do you want playing when you walk into a room feeling fully yourself?

_____
_____
_____
_____
_____

_____

_____

_____

_____

_____

_____

_____

_____

Your healing isn't only about facing shadows. It's about choosing joy, turning the volume up, and remembering you're alive in the middle of it all. Music is prayer, medicine, and permission. So, build your soundtrack. Let it carry you. Let it remind you who you are, not after everything is fixed, but right now, in the beautiful mess of your becoming.

WHICH STAR ARCHETYPE ARE YOU?

1. When inspiration hits, what do you usually do first?

A. Daydream about all the possibilities ●
B. Jump in headfirst, ready to conquer ●
C. Make a plan and organize steps ☀
D. Retreat inward, journal or process alone ☽

2. How do you handle setbacks?

A. I get stuck in "what ifs."
B. I get frustrated, then push harder.
C. I steady myself and keep going, even slowly.
D. I sit in the feelings and mine them for meaning.

3. Which tool would you pack for your healing journey?

A. A sketchbook full of ideas.
B. A torch to light the way forward.
C. A compass to keep me on track.
D. A lantern to explore the shadows.

4. Your friends would describe you as…

A. A dreamer, always imagining new worlds.
B. A firecracker, full of energy and passion.
C. Dependable, steady, the one who shows up.
D. Intuitive, deep, always finding the hidden truths.

5. What's your biggest challenge?

A. Taking action on all my ideas.
B. Burning out before the finish line.
C. Resisting necessary change.
D. Getting lost in the dark too long.

● Mostly A's --> The Dreamer

You live in possibility. Ideas flow easily, but action can feel heavy.
Your gift: Vision.
Your lesson: To trust yourself enough to bring your dreams into form.

◐ Mostly B's--> The Firestarter

You are bold, magnetic, and quick to ignite.
Your gift: Courage.
Your lesson: To pace your flame so you don't burn out before your
brilliance has time to expand.

☀ Mostly C's --> The Steady Flame

You are grounded, reliable, and slow to waver.
Your gift: Stability.
Your lesson: To remember that change is not danger—it's growth.

☽ Mostly D's --> The Shadow Dancer

You feel deeply and navigate the unseen.
Your gift: Depth.
Your lesson: To trust that the dark isn't your enemy—it's where your
wisdom shines.

▨ Reflection Prompt:
Which archetype do you identify with most? Which one do you resist the
most? What does that resistance reveal about where you're growing?

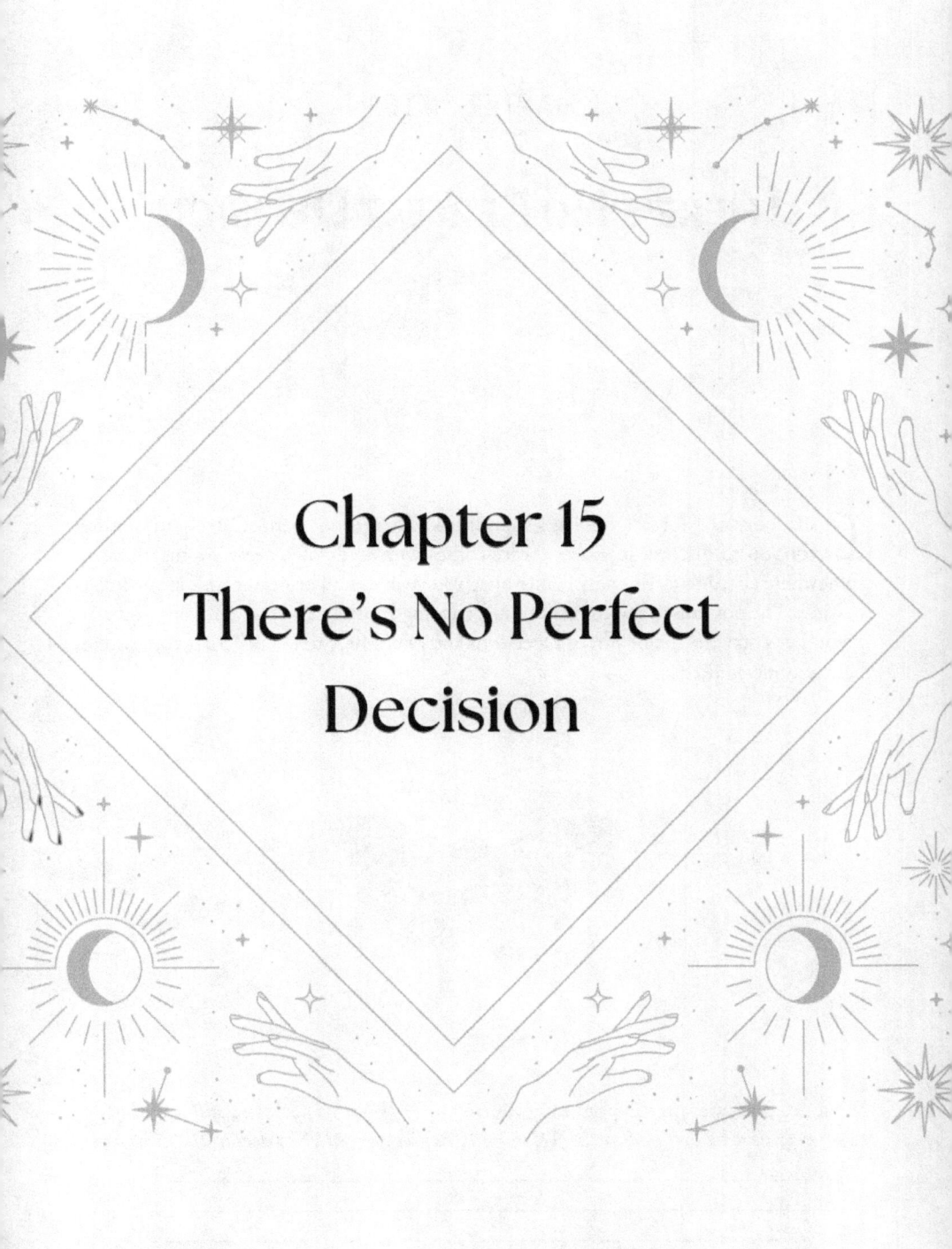

Chapter 15
There's No Perfect Decision

THERE'S NO PERFECT DECISION

Life doesn't have a script, it has a soundtrack. There is no "perfect" decision waiting for you to discover it. Every choice comes with trade-offs, every yes means a no somewhere else, and clarity only comes once you've lived it. The power isn't in getting it flawless. The power is in choosing honestly, trusting yourself, and remembering you can pivot. Let's take the shame out of reflection. You're not here to blame "past" you, you're here to understand her.

What decisions are you still punishing yourself for? "*What's a decision I still second-guess or carry guilt around?*" (*Write the full story. What happened? Why does it still sit heavy?*)

_____

_____

_____

_____

_____

_____
_____
_____
_____
_____
_____
_____
_____
_____
_____
_____
_____
_____
_____
_____
_____
_____
_____
_____
_____
_____
_____

What version of you made that decision? *(How old was I? What did I believe back then? What did I need?)*

_____
_____
_____
_____
_____
_____
_____
_____
_____
_____
_____
_____
_____

What changed after I made that choice (about me, my life, or the situation)?

_____
_____
_____
_____
_____
_____
_____
_____
_____
_____
_____
_____
_____
_____

Am I holding myself to a standard of perfection that no one else is asking of me?

_____
_____
_____
_____
_____
_____
_____
_____
_____
_____
_____
_____
_____
_____

What truth do I know now that I didn't know then?

_____
_____
_____
_____
_____
_____
_____
_____

_____
_____
_____
_____
_____
_____

If you could talk to the version of you who made that choice, what would you say?

_____
_____
_____
_____
_____
_____
_____
_____
_____
_____
_____
_____

What facts have changed since then?

_____
_____
_____
_____
_____
_____
_____
_____
_____
_____
_____

What new choices do you have now?

_____
_____
_____

_____

_____

_____

_____

_____

_____

_____

_____

_____

_____

_____

Which one do you fall into most often when making choices?

☐ Overthinker ("I need the perfect answer")

☐ Avoider ("If I wait long enough, the choice will make itself")

☐ Gut-follower ("I just know when it feels right")

☐ People-pleaser ("I choose what keeps others happy")

☐ Builder ("I'll choose and figure it out as I go")

☐

☐

☐

☐

Realignment Check-In: Let's shift from perfection to permission.

What would it feel like to *bless* that old decision, rather than resent it?

What's a decision I'm currently facing that I've been waiting to get "perfectly right"?

Instead of searching for the "right" answer...
What feels **aligned**?

What feels **rooted in peace?**

What feels **honest, even if uncertain?**

Fill in the Blank

If I trusted myself more, I would stop _____.

If I gave myself permission to pivot, I would _____.

My younger self would be proud that I _____.

Circle One
Which phrase do you need most right now?
☐ "There is no wrong choice."
☐ "I can always choose again."
☐ "Clarity comes through action."
☐ "I trust myself."

Decision Timeline
Think of another "imperfect" decision from your past. Map it in three quick bullet points:

- What you knew *then:*

- What you learned *because of it:*

- What you know *now:*

Write down 3 areas of your life where you're waiting for the "perfect" time or "perfect" clarity to choose. Then ask yourself: *What's the smallest step of courage I could take here instead?*

_____
_____
_____
_____
_____
_____
_____
_____
_____
_____
_____
_____
_____
_____

_____
_____
_____
_____
_____
_____
_____
_____
_____
_____
_____
_____

_____
_____
_____
_____

_____
_____
_____
_____
_____
_____
_____
_____
_____
_____

Talk to Her
Write a note to your past self, the version of you who made a decision you still carry.
Start with: "
Hey babe, I know why you chose what you did... ▢

_____
_____
_____
_____
_____
_____
_____
_____
_____
_____
_____
_____
_____
_____
_____
_____
_____
_____
_____
_____
_____
_____
_____
_____
_____

Reframe the Fear

Fear says: "What if I choose wrong again?"

You say: _____

(Write your new truth. One sentence. Make it strong.)

Recommitment Ritual

Circle one word that you want to carry with you into your next decision:

Clarity / Courage / Trust / Alignment / Grace / Presence / Flow / Self-Compassion

Now finish this sentence:

"I commit to choosing from _____, not from fear."

You don't need the perfect answer. You need the courage to decide, the trust to pivot, and the grace to keep moving. Every choice teaches you something you couldn't have learned otherwise. Every path, even the detours, grows you. Stop punishing yourself for not predicting the future. You're not supposed to. You're here to build it, one decision, one moment, one brave step at a time.

You're not making a forever decision. You're making a now one—with the power to pivot, evolve, and choose again.

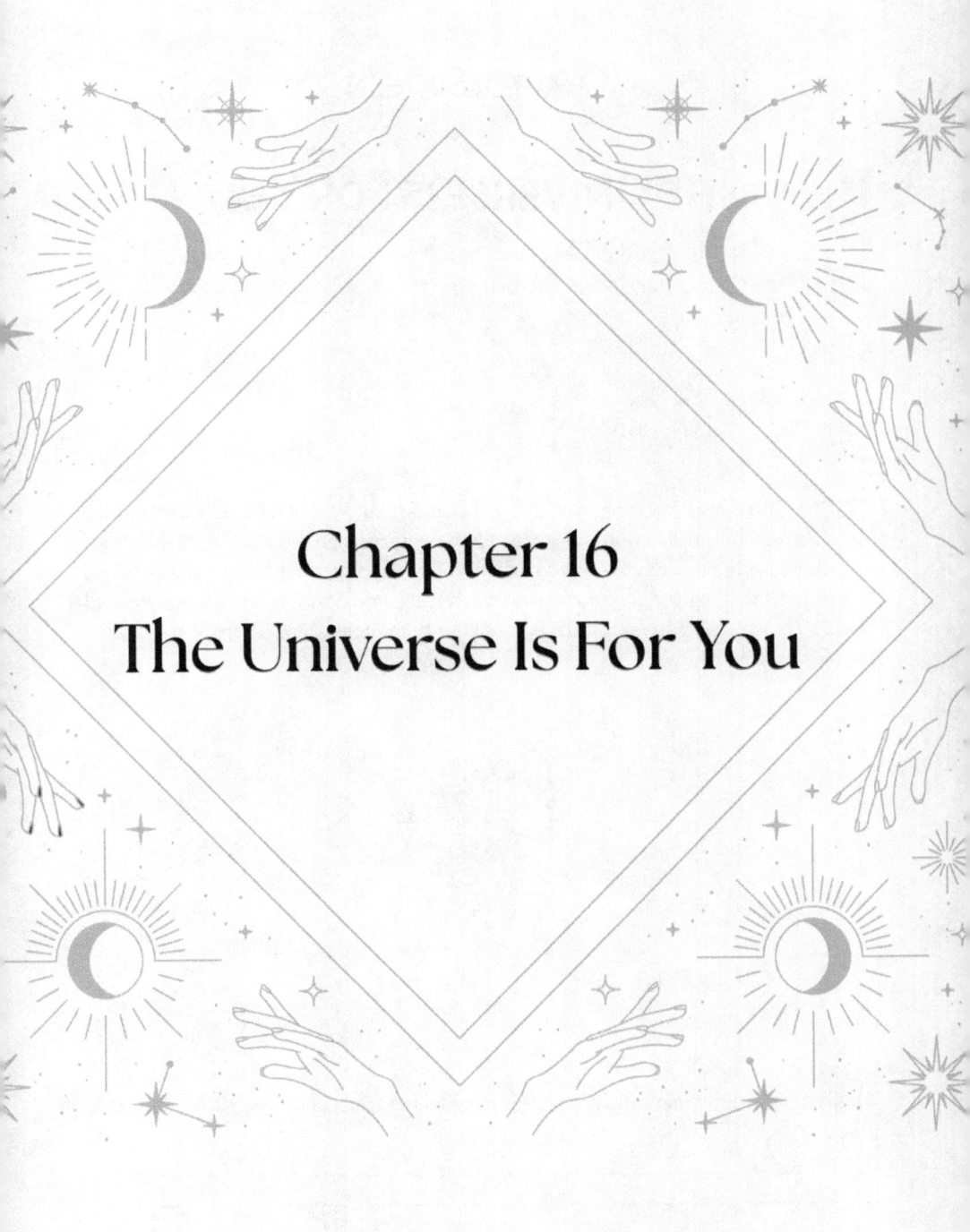

Chapter 16
The Universe Is For You

Chapter Sixteen

The Universe is For You

The Universe isn't testing you... it's positioning you. What looks like a detour may actually be the direction. What feels like delay may be protection. Trust isn't about everything being easy; it's choosing to believe you're supported even in the chaos. When you stop demanding perfection and start co-creating, you begin to see that every closed door, every whisper, every reroute is part of your becoming. The Universe is not against you. It's for you. Always.

Think about a time you thought everything was falling apart, but it was really falling into place.

_____
_____
_____
_____
_____

What "detour" ended up becoming the most aligned path?

What felt like a breakdown, but turned into a breakthrough?

What moments felt like devastation but became a doorway?

_____
_____
_____
_____
_____
_____
_____
_____
_____
_____
_____
_____
_____

What would you do differently if you believed, without a doubt, that the Universe was on your side today?

_____
_____
_____
_____
_____
_____
_____
_____
_____
_____
_____
_____
_____
_____
_____
_____

Fill in the Blank

The last time I felt rerouted, I thought it meant _____, but now I see _____.

When I look back, the hardest season of my life taught me

_____.

If the Universe whispered one word to me today, it would be

_____.

Check One
When the Universe feels silent, how do you usually respond?
□ Panic and assume I'm failing
□ Push harder to prove myself
□ Numb out and avoid it
□ Pause and listen for the whisper
□ Remind myself that silence is still guidance

Draw It Out
Sketch (or doodle) a symbol that represents "trust" to you. Don't overthink it... maybe it's a bridge, a hand, a spiral, or just a word in bold letters. This becomes your reminder that you don't walk alone.

Scavenger Hunt for Signs
The rest of today and all of tomorrow, keep your eyes open for "small signals" ...repeating numbers, animals, songs, overheard words, unexpected pauses. Write them down here. (take notes on your phone if you need to, then copy them over.) Notice patterns. Ask: *What could this mean for me right now?*

Signs Log

Instructions:
This is your place to capture the little nudges, synchronicities, and whispers you notice. They might seem small (numbers, animals, songs, phrases, conversations, delays) but

together they tell a story. Track them. See what repeats. Reflect on what they might be showing you.

Date | Sign/Signal | Where I Saw It | What It Might Mean

_____

_____

_____

_____

_____

_____

_____

_____

_____

_____

_____

_____

_____

_____

_____

_____

_____

_____

_____

_____

_____

_____

_____

_____

_____

_____

Journal Sparks

Where in my life am I still interpreting delays as punishment instead of protection?

_____

_____

_____

_____

_____

_____

_____
_____
_____
_____
_____
_____
_____

What would shift if I stopped praying for open doors and instead chose to walk the hallway?

_____
_____
_____
_____
_____
_____
_____
_____
_____
_____
_____
_____
_____

If I trusted the Universe was building my landing, what risks would I finally take?

_____
_____
_____
_____
_____
_____
_____
_____
_____
_____
_____
_____

Tiny Trust Practices

These are not about *doing more*. They're about *believing deeper*. Check any that feel supportive right now, or write in your own:

Write "The Universe is for me" on a sticky note and put it where you'll see it daily
Go for a walk and ask the Universe to show you a sign of alignment (perhaps a butterfly or lizard)
Reframe one frustrating moment today into a message of redirection
Start a "Proof List" of times you were rerouted into something better
Sit in silence for 3 minutes and ask, "What's shifting in me right now?"

_____

_____

The Universe is not waiting to see if you'll fail. It's walking ahead, building your landing before you even leap. Every reroute, every whisper, every pause is part of the plan. Stop demanding certainty before you move. Start living like you're supported, because you are.

YOUR ORACLE
PULL

Pick a number that calls to you.
Flip to the back to reveal your message.

Chapter 17
Grey Days and Alignment

GREY DAYS AND ALIGNMENT

G rey Days don't always come with tears or chaos. They sneak in quietly, dimming your energy, making everything feel "off." They're not flaws, they're flags. A whisper from your body and the Universe that you need to pause, soften, or realign. If ignored, the whispers become roars: burnout, breakdown, or breaking points. Alignment isn't always loud or joyful at first, sometimes it feels like grief or disruption. But when you honor the signals, even the fog becomes guidance, and slowly, life starts to feel like yours again.

What does stress feel like in your body?

_____
_____
_____
_____
_____
_____
_____
_____
_____
_____
_____
_____
_____
_____

How can you recognize the signs earlier?

_____

_____
_____
_____
_____
_____
_____
_____
_____
_____
_____
_____
_____
_____

What commitments are currently draining you?

_____
_____
_____
_____
_____
_____
_____
_____
_____
_____
_____
_____
_____

Where have you been choosing peacekeeping over peacemaking?

_____
_____
_____
_____
_____
_____
_____
_____
_____
_____

_____
_____
_____

What would it look like to disappoint others in order to honor yourself?

_____
_____
_____
_____
_____
_____
_____
_____
_____
_____
_____
_____
_____
_____
_____

Creative Exercises

Grey Day Scale
On a scale of 1–10, where do you usually notice yourself on a Grey Day?

1 = I don't even notice it's happening until I crash

5 = I notice but push through anyway

10 = I name it and give myself grace right away

Grey Day Bingo *(check all that apply)*

☐ Snapping over small things

☐ Forgetting why I walked into a room

☐ Coffee doesn't taste right

☐ Hoodie + couch all day

☐ Everything feels loud *and* too quiet

☐ Performing "I'm fine" while empty inside

☐ Zero motivation but impossible to rest

Body Map Prompt

Draw a simple outline of a body. Mark where stress or misalignment usually shows up for you (headache, chest tightness, stomachache, etc.). Then, next to each area, write a soothing action you could take.

Two-Column Grid

Peacekeeping (keeping others happy) vs. *Peacemaking (honoring my truth)*

Example:

Peacekeeping: Saying yes to another obligation → Peacemaking: Canceling to protect my energy.

Quick Reflection Prompts

What are my earliest "grey flags" (tiny signs I'm heading into burnout)?

_____
_____
_____
_____
_____
_____
_____
_____
_____
_____
_____
_____
_____
_____

Who in my life gives me permission to rest, and how can I lean into that?

_____
_____
_____
_____
_____
_____
_____
_____
_____
_____
_____
_____
_____

What space or ritual (like my garage, playlists, or meditation) helps me recalibrate fastest?

_____
_____
_____
_____
_____
_____
_____

_____
_____
_____
_____
_____
_____

Grey Days are not weakness. They're whispers. They're sacred signals that your soul needs gentleness, your body needs pause, and your spirit needs space to realign. You don't have to bulldoze through the fog. You're allowed to soften, slow down, and reset. Alignment isn't always loud, but it is always available.

Write a letter to your body: *"What have you been trying to tell me that I've been ignoring?"*
_____
_____
_____
_____
_____
_____
_____
_____
_____
_____
_____
_____
_____

Circle three areas (work, family, friendships, health, creativity, etc.) and rate them on a scale of 1–10 for how aligned they feel today. Where's the gap?
_____
_____
_____
_____
_____
_____
_____
_____
_____
_____
_____

_____

_____

_____

Write one "alignment non-negotiable" — something you will protect no matter what (rest, joy, boundaries, creativity, movement, etc.).

_____

_____

_____

_____

_____

_____

_____

_____

_____

_____

_____

Finish this sentence: _"If I was living in full alignment right now, I would…"_☐

_____

_____

_____

_____

_____

_____

_____

_____

_____

_____

_____

_____

_____

Think of alignment as a triangle with three points: **Body, Breath, and Boundaries.** When you reset all three, you realign.

Step 1: Body (Presence)

☐ Put one hand on your chest, one on your stomach. Close your eyes.
☐ Ask: *Where am I holding tension?* Move or stretch that part gently.
☐ Write: *"My body feels..."* (let it be honest, not polished).

Step 2: Breath (Clarity)

☐ Inhale for 4, hold for 4, exhale for 6. Repeat three times.
☐ Whisper (out loud if you can): *"I'm here now."*
☐ Write: *"Right now, I need..."* (a nap, water, less noise, a hug, quiet).

Step 3: Boundaries (Choice)

☐ Look at your to-do list. Cross off one thing that doesn't actually need you today.
☐ Say: *"It's safe to release this."*
☐ Write: *"One way I will protect my energy today is..."*

he messy middle

```
                  O A W G K Z T T I I
                S A E U Y J X F O N C R V A J C
              W N S M U I E F O G Z D X E E G E G E L
            E V V N E V G L P N E L E M N D G V R G N N
          D N U Y J S M Y Q S I F W A Y W H C R A I Z K R N P
        G O Z V R R Q N Z F B P Q U V P Y Y T A X T T A O B V B
      U J M U X U E R B Q A I J U O M A E L D D I M Y S S E M R X
    P S J I G H T C K C X F L I K G O U N M L E P H S W G X X I U C
    P K T H F E E A C K S J L M W B N S Z D C G I E P L A S O U S W
  A C C B R D E C L O T P S A G U H A E J E E E P H C A P P M L M T Y
  J K W K K J G J N I M U E Z F R L H T V X A K M X B S T I L L N E S S Y
  X X H L I H A H E B W U P N U H A G K P J B S G Q W E S L V X D N Q J A
Y T H D O M I B L S R D S X G D R W U E R E W M Z J T K H T P R G P U R Q Z
V X A X Z N D U S E A E E N Q E E R O N W R D E Z Z Q G P Y D E E R O A G R
A M Q M J R E P S R T A I B D W M R R P W S Y R Y W U V O I X S G O J L R O
X F U T I M Z Q S X P E L M N N C G D H A Z C O S I I S V S L H I R C B I A C D
C R Z W F Y C F D T N A V E S A E Z C T R C X O A D O Z T Y W L L W E V G W K T
U I T N A G T B Z P E P R N L T O Z L K G S R K E H V J U D K K I Z S M N S B W
J M X A V D W B Z H T R Z I T H T B R A F F T O R I C X Y P Y M E E S S M U O Z
C P A R C Q L C N N U T O I Z C K K E E C A I E H O N V J N W I N J Z R E B T Y
G K Z J V I D X G S S F K C N F R P S R H I K V C J Q Z N U R L C G R Y N Z T E
T X D D B M J R M U J D W J F L R U E B P H E G B E B L W S N H E V Z N T S O R
D H T U U Z E W R D G D I M R Y Y A T V G Z X R Y S Z K O A W J Q F N O S Y M U
C M I C R I O T S W M Y G V O V G X K Y U X Z D A V O W D F M X U G U A J F W S
L I E R W I S Y M U W L T I T Q R B Y X T B K R A P A A K V L X A X L T Y U P Q
H M S U E S O O R A L W R S W E N N S Z O J F L H H Y A I P G D E W Z F I Y
Y U A P J M E P V I P E X I T Y B E E M N J U H H D T E X S K D W G L R I D
T X H O K H Y R O T I B L N D D G Q E A K J G S K I J R B P F N M D A H F F
S F U V M U A R I V N N Z V A G V S W F T K J Q Q A B D I N M E L D I O
O G O A H V U Q N E P F E G Y U J D X T I F S O N Q I T R E Z Z V M Z B
H X D E N O Q Q G D A D E S J N Z G O Q E O L U S E N L A K Y T I C O
C K K Q I S W B X Q F I R K L X L O B I B P H I G A G L O O R D F C
B X E U T C R O G O V E W B X W P A U V N Y I Z I J M H E Z J Y
V I S A L D V Y X M Y F F A M D L Q M R I T J G C K E N T A
M P O Z U A L K L A B R T Q S A Y W W A T S Q J W G V F
G L R H L H L E L W W L V H N B B E C O M I N G O G
G F S D U L V V W F Z C M C V T G R A R Z M N R
N V A H S X J S K R Y E B L F Y B H H F
X S C G O D M G C A Q X K W O K
R F D Y F B C N B O
```

WORD LIST

ALIGNMENT	GREY DAY	PRESENCE	SPIRAL
BALANCE	GRIT	PROCESS	STILLNESS
BECOMING	GUIDE	RAW	SURRENDER
BREAKDOWN	HEALING	RECALIBRATE	TENDER
BREAKTHROUGH	HONEST	RESET	TRUST
CHAOS	INBETWEEN	RESILIENCE	WAITING
DEPTH	LAYERS	RISE	
FALL	MESSYMIDDLE	ROCKBOTTOM	
FOG	PAUSE	SPIRAL	

Chapter 18
The Outsider Friend

THE OUTSIDER FRIEND

Not everyone is wired for constant connection, and that doesn't make you less of a friend. Being the "outsider" doesn't mean being unwanted, it means you move differently. You show up deeply, in seasons, in moments that matter. You're a bridge, not a spotlight-seeker. Your presence can be quieter, less frequent, and still profoundly meaningful. Your friendship doesn't have to look like everyone else's to matter.

Where have you felt like an outsider in your relationships?

_____

_____

_____

_____

_____

_____

_____

_____

_____

_____

_____

_____

_____

_____

What would it feel like to release the pressure to perform connection?

_____

_____

_____

_____

_____

_____

_____

_____

_____

_____

_____

_____

_____

Who in your life loves you without needing all of you, all the time?

_____

_____

_____

_____

_____

_____

_____

_____

_____

_____

_____

_____

_____

_____

Creative Exercises

Check One
Which description of friendship feels most true for you right now?
☐ Everyday connection — constant touchpoints and messages
☐ Seasonal connection — strong in certain moments or eras
☐ Situational connection — specific contexts (work, sports, parenting)
☐ Bridge connection — moving between circles, holding space in between
☐ Lone wolf — few close ties, but depth in the ones that remain

Fill in the Blank

I feel most loved when my friends _____.

I feel safe offering friendship when I know _____.

The kind of friend I want to be remembered as is _____.

Check Boxes
Which of these resonate with you as your "outsider strengths"?
☐ I see people who feel invisible
☐ I show up powerfully in the hard moments
☐ I connect people across groups or seasons
☐ I love deeply without needing constant proof
☐ I offer presence over performance

Gentle Release Exercise
Write down one "rule of friendship" you've been carrying that doesn't serve you (e.g., "Good friends always respond right away" or "I have to be at every birthday"). Then, cross it out and rewrite a new truth that honors the way *you* love.

_____

_____

_____

_____

_____

_____

_____

_____

_____

_____

_____

_____

_____

Doodle Prompt

Draw (or sketch) a symbol for the way you show up in friendships. Maybe it's a bridge, a lighthouse, a thread, or even a quiet star. Let the image remind you that your way is valid.

You don't need to be the loudest or the most available to matter. Your love doesn't expire because it's quiet, seasonal, or imperfect. The way you show up (real, intentional, and true) is enough. Connection isn't measured by frequency, but by presence.

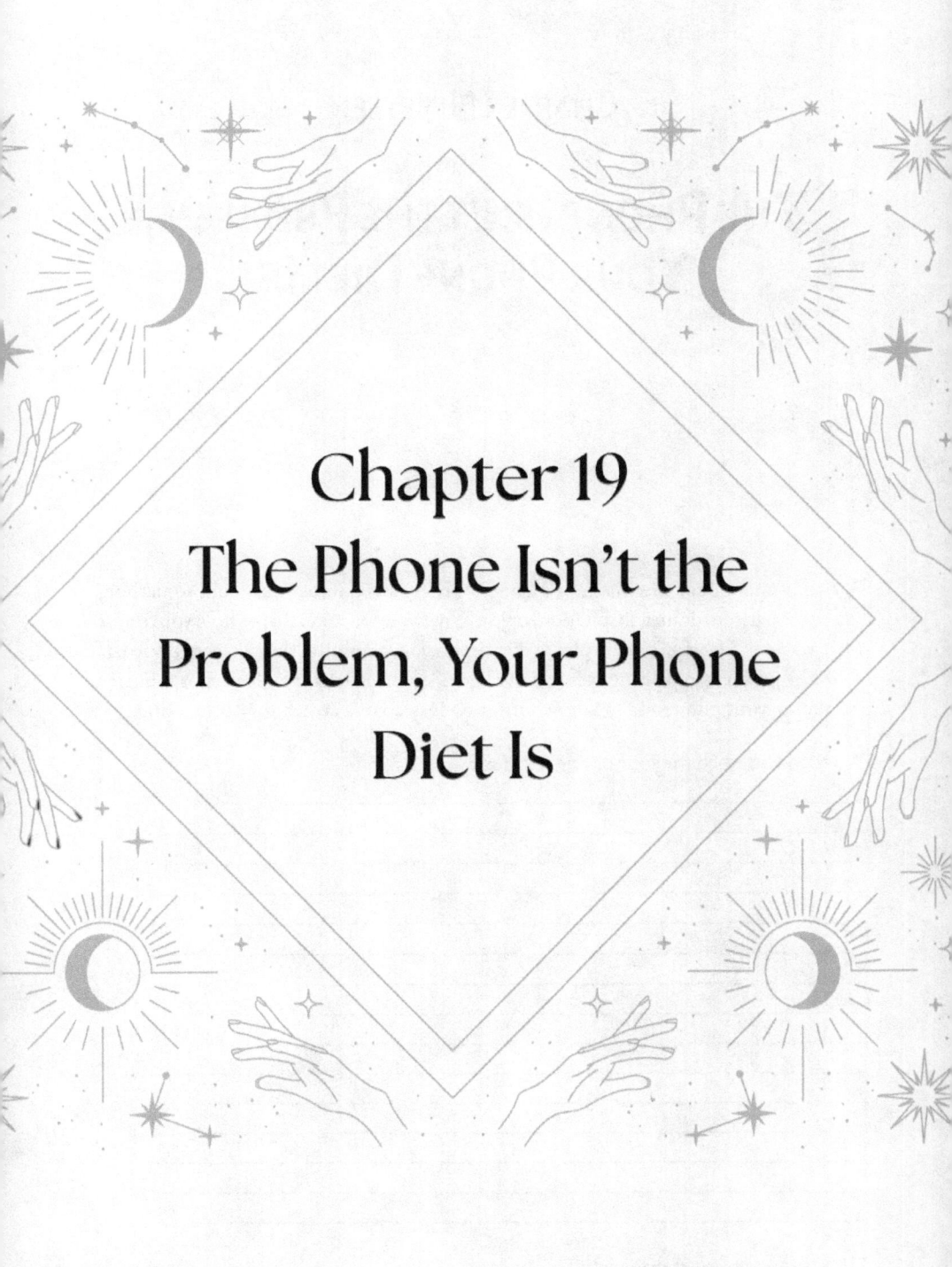

Chapter 19
The Phone Isn't the Problem, Your Phone Diet Is

THE PHONE ISN'T THE PROBLEM, YOUR PHONE DIET IS

Your phone isn't the villain. It's a mirror. Every scroll feeds your mind something... comparison, drama, inspiration, or joy. What you consume shapes how you feel, and what you avoid facing. A toxic phone diet drains you; a mindful one can actually expand you. The power is in pausing before you plug in, curating what you feed your mind, and reclaiming your phone as a tool for connection instead of a crutch for distraction.

What do you reach for your phone for most?

_____
_____
_____
_____
_____
_____
_____
_____
_____
_____
_____
_____
_____
_____
_____
_____

How do you feel after using it?

_____

_____
_____
_____
_____
_____
_____
_____
_____
_____
_____
_____
_____
_____
_____

What content makes you feel energized, and what makes you feel small?

_____
_____
_____
_____
_____
_____
_____
_____
_____
_____
_____
_____
_____

Where can you set new boundaries for yourself or your family?

_____
_____
_____
_____
_____
_____
_____
_____
_____
_____

_____
_____
_____

What creative outlet have you replaced with scrolling?

_____
_____
_____
_____
_____
_____
_____
_____
_____
_____
_____
_____
_____

Phone Diet Checkup
Check all that apply:
☐ I scroll before I get out of bed
☐ I check my phone during meals
☐ I lose track of time when "just checking"
☐ I feel worse about myself after scrolling
☐ I scroll to avoid silence or hard feelings
☐ I compare myself more than I connect

Swap It Grid

Current Habit —> Gentle Swap

Scrolling in bed at night—>Reading 1 page of a book / listening to calming music

Checking phone in bathroom—>Deep breathing or gratitude thought

Opening apps on autopilot—>Leaving home screen blank / moving apps to folders

Midday scroll for "escape"—>Step outside / stretch / short walk

Posting for validation—>Calling or texting one safe friend

Add your own here:

Fill in the Blank

My most nourishing use of my phone is _____.

My most draining use of my phone is _____.

One app I'd be healthier without is _____.

One creator who always inspires me is _____.

Phone-Free Zones (circle or add your own)
☐ Meals
☐ Bedroom
☐ Family time
☐ First 30 minutes of the day
☐ In the car (parked or driving)
☐ After 9 PM

Witness vs. Performance Prompt
Where have I been posting for *performance* instead of *connection*?

_____
_____
_____
_____
_____
_____
_____
_____
_____
_____

_____
_____
_____
_____
_____

What would it look like to be witnessed in real life instead?
_____
_____
_____
_____
_____
_____
_____
_____
_____
_____
_____
_____
_____

You don't need to throw away your phone, you need to change your diet. When you unfollow what drains you, mute what makes you feel small, and pause before you plug in, your phone stops being a pacifier and becomes a tool of expansion. Reclaim your feed, and you reclaim your energy.

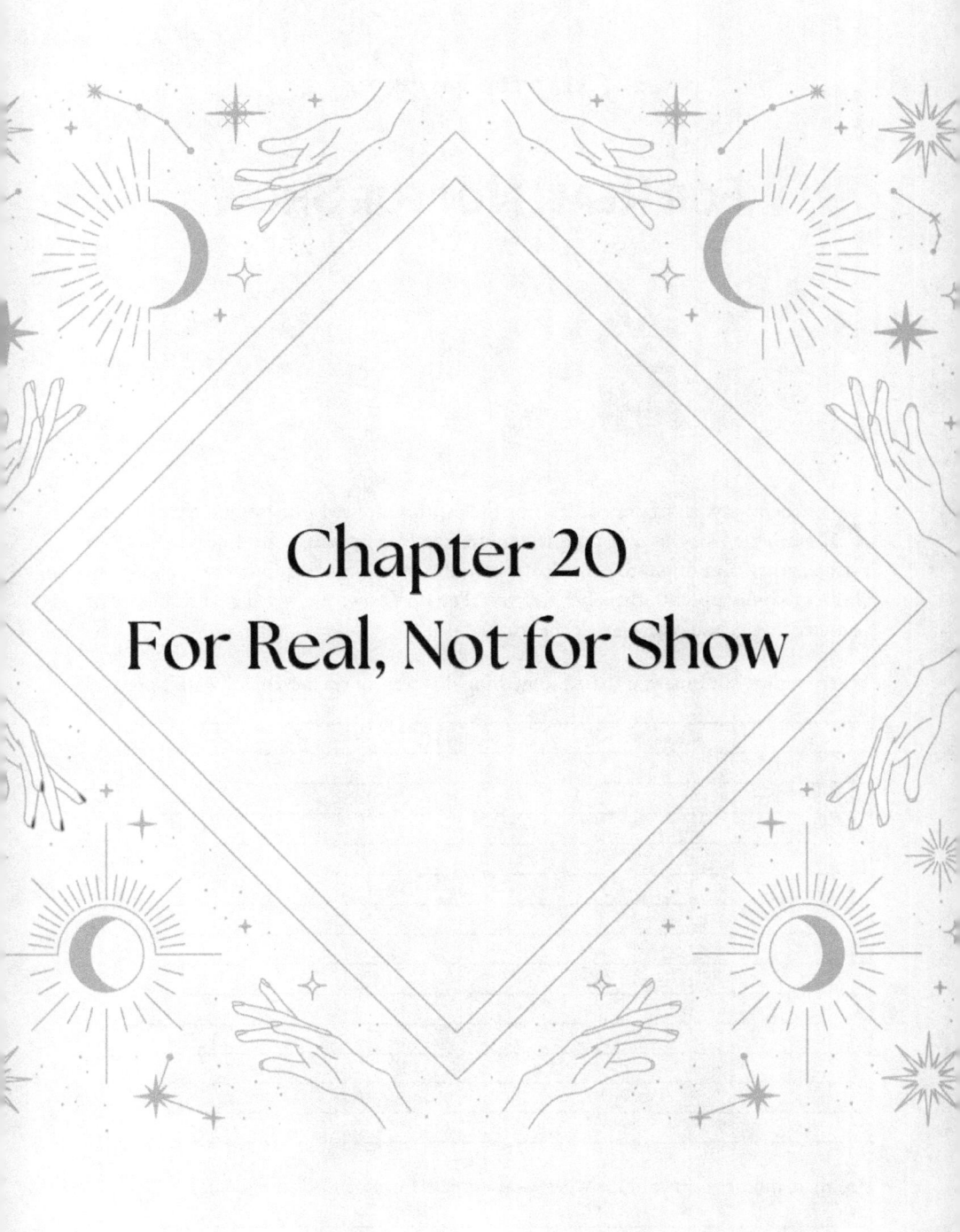

Chapter 20
For Real, Not for Show

CHAPTER TWENTY

FOR REAL, NOT FOR SHOW

Authenticity isn't curated. It's not the caption dressed in hashtags, the "healing aesthetic," or the post polished enough to earn applause. Real healing is often private, gritty, and unphotogenic. It happens in silence, in breakdowns no one sees, in choices that disappoint others but free you. You don't owe the world a performance of your becoming. You owe yourself the truth.

When was the last time you shared something that was for real...even if it wasn't pretty?

_____
_____
_____
_____
_____
_____
_____
_____
_____
_____
_____
_____
_____
_____

Are there moments in your life where you were performing instead of being?

_____
_____
_____

_____
_____
_____
_____
_____
_____
_____
_____
_____
_____
_____
_____

What would it look like to share your story without needing applause?

_____
_____
_____
_____
_____
_____
_____
_____
_____
_____
_____
_____
_____

What part of your healing is just for you?

_____
_____
_____
_____
_____
_____
_____
_____
_____
_____
_____

_____

_____

Truth Cards
Write three "truths" you've been carrying quietly.

Cross It Out
Write down one performance or "curated" version of yourself you've been showing the world.

Now cross it out — boldly. Underneath, write the unfiltered truth.

Circle One
When I feel pressure to *perform healing*, I usually:
☐ Post instead of call
☐ Caption instead of cry
☐ Soften instead of speak
☐ Hide instead of risk being misunderstood

Fill in the Blank

My most sacred, private healing moment was _____.

I feel most real when I _____.

The part of me I'm still protecting is _____.

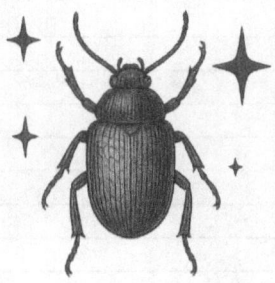

Doodle Prompt
Sketch an image that represents your "armor" — then draw how it would look if you set it down.

Where in your life are you still trying to "look okay" even when you're not? What would it cost to drop the act? What might it set free?

_____
_____
_____
_____
_____
_____
_____
_____
_____
_____
_____
_____
_____
_____
_____
_____

Think of a time you were quietly unraveling while the world thought you were doing great. How did that season shape you? What would the *real* caption have said?

_____
_____
_____
_____
_____
_____
_____
_____
_____
_____
_____
_____
_____
_____

Finish this sentence without trying to make it pretty:

The version of me I don't let people see is...

Now ask: What does *she* need from you right now?

Affirmations

I don't need to be seen to be valid.
My growth doesn't need to be pretty. It just needs to be mine.
I choose truth over performance.
I am safe to show up as I am...unfiltered, unpolished, and real.
I don't perform my healing. I live it.

The most powerful parts of you may never be witnessed by an audience... and that's the point. Your becoming doesn't need applause to be real. Some of your deepest healing will live in silence, in solitude, in the quiet places only you and the Universe will ever know. And that's more than enough.

stepping into power

```
        M Q R G V O                                    H E U S W O
      U Q V M J Y M A Y                              B M Z Y E X B F Y
    Q P V L D P O W E R A                          H B U Y F H J V M P S
    Q L D S G T W O L F U B K                      C J A H R W A V C A N O J
  N T W A J I S G X O V S U H C                  M O A R T J W H V K C Z K B U
  Q X C M P J N C T B P K F S O                  L Q D U W F P G G Q P R B Y X
U X R V G Q I R L D B K F R M U K            P Q E V A T R N S M E D T B L D D
W E U K O L K G Y P H V D E X R Q K        B S W P Z A Y H J G C P W C H U S F
D A A S A P X P Z B I Q X E R A B D A E Y Z B C D L H E J M Y F G T B S G
Z Z Y E Z V A N H O O U G D W G I Q K W P V R L I K I R N K S G D Q V A K
L M H X I N Z I C I M L N O N E E O C U O W K G V T X G X T L F Y X I Z G
V X C L G L M O Z X E E D M O U Q M V Q L R U W T Q E P N L I F C R W T L
R Q Z G Q B O O X B R N S S B M F Y R F G S T P E Y U N G M I C M I V Y W
A O U S D A K B R F A E V Y F M I K G M J I J H H E B T G S E J H X V R Z
O A R E J S T W Z O T S E F O Q X Z S R H N U R Y D H S Q A G N B H L S I
N L C F I O M Q B T I W S E W I U X B E N O A D K U U O T M O T S T V
C H I E O D H H W L V L H K D N Z P O O N R I X M S R P K V O S K G K
J F O J V V W I D E V T S F I C F L U K W E Q S N K T T Z Z T Y Q Q U
  O V V S A J I P I K F L R A P L D N Z I K A Z N E C N A I D A R H
  Z G G V K R W O F V K F F O B F N D F D R D D R A R L N L N R X V
    A Z N Z O B H H D R I S B O R Y A M X L I F T R P V H X N L S
    E U H Y W Z D G P E H F A Z H M R R D W A S L T X X A S B W E
    R S Y S C W U R Y H F S Y Z O I U J I E I I U F S E E K C
    Y V E U W Y C F Y G Z Y L L N E Y U A G U L N Z D U R S U
      T Z O D E P S Y T I X M A X S T B H L R Z C G H F F X
      P L R K R K D H N L P T I K E T Y F M G O C T B W
    J K J R R L G A T G Y E N C J W H O L E S F P I Y
      P T S H U J R U I E N O U G H A W B R E B B T
      V S A L S O I F Y Y I H V P O E M U N N O
        T T O G L T H Q M T Q G R D X L F O X
        M R X Q I Y B Z A C D H X A O I A
          Z U N O F O Q R Q T T C W Q Y
          A T N L I C E C Z T Y W Z
          S H U N J B Y Q N J S
          O G U E I Y Y T F
          N H L L L V E
          W O N T S
            S Z J
              T
```

WORD LIST

ALIGNMENT	ENOUGH	LIBERATION	TRUST
AUTHENTIC	EXPANSION	LIGHT	TRUTH
BOLD	FIERCE	MAGNETIC	VOICE
BOUNDARIES	FLOW	POWER	WHOLE
BRAVE	FREEDOM	RADIANCE	WORTHY
COURAGE	HEALING	RISING	
ENERGY	INTUITION	SACRED	

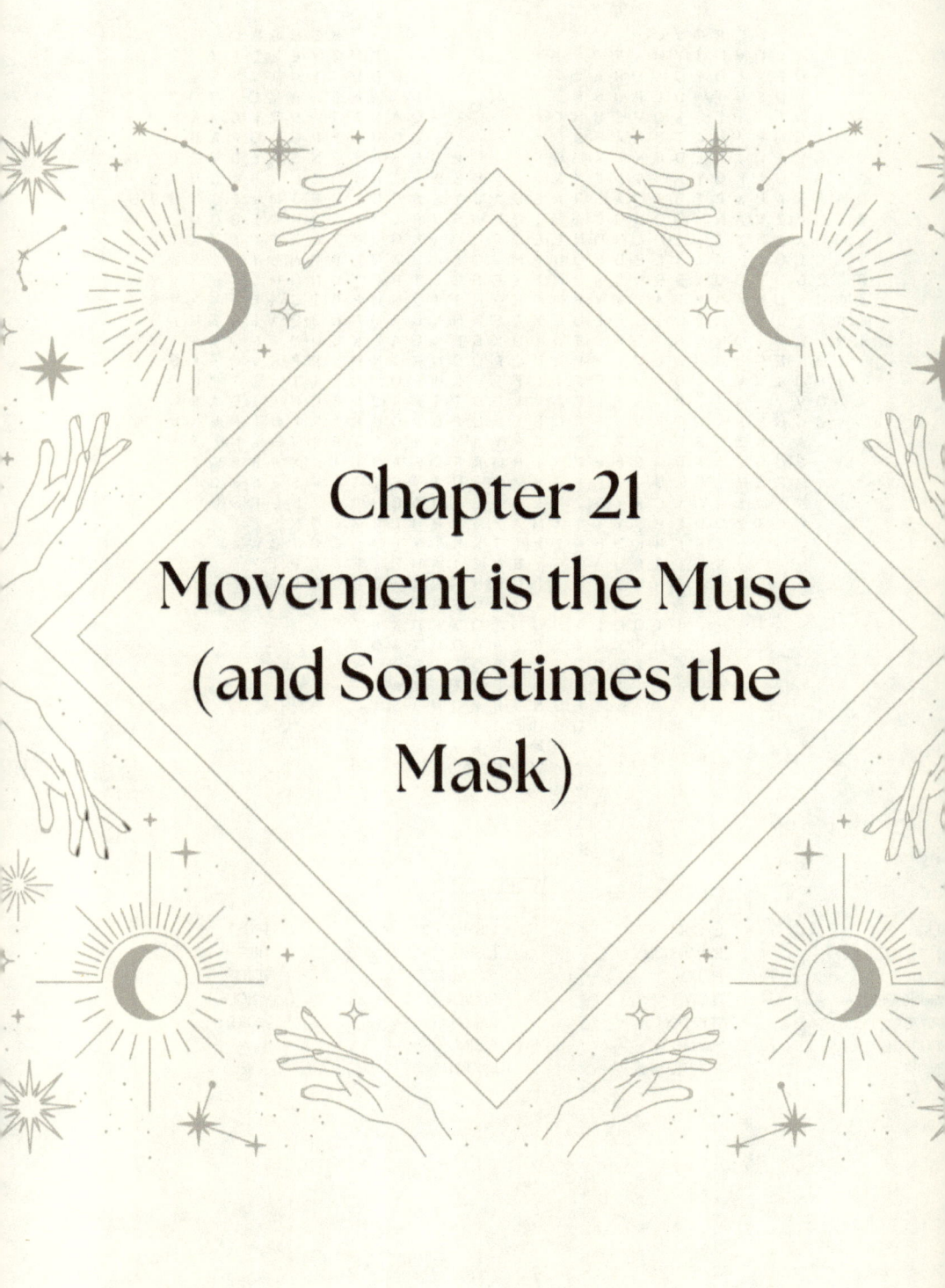

Chapter 21
Movement is the Muse (and Sometimes the Mask)

CHAPTER TWENTY-ONE

MOVEMENT IS THE MUSE (AND SOMETIMES THE MASK)

C larity doesn't arrive in silence... it meets you in motion. Inspiration isn't waiting for perfect conditions, it shows up in chaos, in halfway ideas, in the middle of life. But not all movement is medicine. Sometimes it heals, sometimes it hides. The key is intention: moving toward what expands you instead of away from what you're afraid to feel. You don't need perfect plans. You just need to move.

What would 10 minutes of intentional movement look like today?

_____

_____

_____

_____

_____

_____
_____
_____
_____
_____
_____
_____
_____
_____

Where have I been waiting for perfection when I could just take a step?

_____
_____
_____
_____
_____
_____
_____
_____
_____
_____
_____
_____
_____

What's one thing I could do for 5 minutes that moves this forward?

_____
_____
_____
_____
_____
_____
_____
_____
_____
_____
_____
_____
_____

Where have I been using chaos as a distraction instead of a catalyst?

_____
_____
_____
_____
_____
_____
_____
_____
_____
_____
_____
_____
_____

What space (garage, car, walk, etc.) can I designate as my "movement portal" ... the place ideas get to flow?

_____
_____
_____
_____
_____
_____
_____
_____
_____
_____
_____
_____
_____
_____

Chaos Notebook Challenge
Keep a notebook (or Notes app) nearby. Capture sparks _exactly as they come_ — messy, half-finished, unedited.
Prompt: Write the last thought you almost ignored.

Momentum Tracker
Instead of listing unfinished tasks, track *what you did move forward today*:
☐ Sent the email
☐ Wrote the sentence
☐ Walked around the block
☐ Jotted the idea
☐ Took the next tiny step

Circle One
When I feel stuck, the best medicine is usually:
☐ Move my body
☐ Move my space (declutter, shift furniture, light a candle)
☐ Move my mind (brain dump, voice memo)

5-Minute Dares: Pick one (or make your own):
Dance to a full song in your kitchen
Voice memo a thought instead of overthinking it
Step outside barefoot and breathe deeply
Write the ugliest paragraph you can (no editing)
Clean one corner of a room while asking, "What else in my life wants clarity?"

Fill in the Blank

My chaos often sparks _____.

When I'm in motion, I feel _____.

If I stopped right now, the truth I might hear is _____.

Affirmations
I don't need a perfect space. I just need space.
I trust inspiration to meet me in motion.
Small steps are still steps.
I make magic in the middle of the mess.
Momentum is medicine.

Movement doesn't demand grace, it demands honesty. Messy, clumsy, chaotic action is still sacred if it keeps you connected to yourself. The muse doesn't need silence; she just needs you to move.

Across

4 The heavy stories we tell ourselves on repeat.

5 A day when everything feels muted.

6 What grows when you stop dimming your light.

10 What you risk by being too polished.

12 The currency we build beyond money.

13 What perfectionism secretly protects: fear of ____

14 The practice of softening instead of forcing.

15 The inner compass that guides when logic wont.

Down

1 Does this bring me ___ or take my ___

2 Am I sharing this for truth or for ___?

3 The currency more valuable than dolla

4 The emotional fog that signals misalignment.

7 The practice of choosing joy even whe feels heavy.

8 The inner critic who polices your joy. _____ adult

9 What you should choose over approva

11 The voice that whispers, You're not rea

Chapter 22
Open Hands (Control)

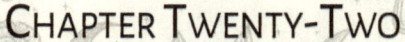

CHAPTER TWENTY-TWO

OPEN HANDS (CONTROL)

Control feels safe... but it's also heavy. We grip outcomes, timelines, and appearances because we're afraid of what will happen if we let go. But true growth doesn't happen in the grip. It happens in the release. Surrender isn't weakness. It's trust. It's unclenching your fists so the Universe can place something better in them.

Where in my life am I micromanaging outcomes?

_____

_____

_____

_____

_____

_____

_____

_____

_____

_____

_____

_____

_____

_____

What would it feel like to loosen my grip, even slightly?

_____

_____

_____

_____
_____
_____
_____
_____
_____
_____
_____
_____
_____
_____

What's one situation where I could practice letting go this week?

_____
_____
_____
_____
_____
_____
_____
_____
_____
_____
_____
_____

When have I surrendered before and received more than I expected?

_____
_____
_____
_____
_____
_____
_____
_____
_____
_____
_____
_____
_____

Root Before You Rise: "Bamboo doesn't rush. It roots." Without rushing to bloom, what can you **root into** right now?

□ Patience
□ Trust
□ Stillness
□ A new habit or mindset
□ Support (even if it's hard to receive)
□ Being seen, even if it scares you

Circle or write your own: _____

Now, write one sentence that grounds you in that root.

    "I   root   into   ___ _____   because
___ _____ ."

Fill in the Blank

I try to control _____ because deep down I fear
_____ .

If I let go, I believe_____ might happen.

But if I trusted, I believe _____ could open instead.

Circle One
When I imagine loosening control, the first feeling that rises in me is:
□ Relief
□ Panic
□ Curiosity
□ Resistance

□ Open Hands Practice

Step 1: Trace Your Hand
On the next page, place your hands down flat and trace around them. Don't worry about perfection — messy is real, messy is enough.

Step 2: Name the Grip
Inside your traced hands, write down the things you're still clenching tight:

Timelines you want to control
Outcomes you're afraid of losing
Identities you feel pressured to keep up
The fears you don't want anyone to see

Step 3: Name the Release
Outside your traced hands, write what you're ready to loosen:

"I release the need to know when it happens."
"I release carrying the weight for everyone else."
"I release the shame of not having it all together."

Step 4: Let It Breathe
Doodle around your hands — roots, waves, stars, bamboo, whatever feels right. This is you creating space. This is you showing your body what surrender looks like.

What surprised me as I wrote inside my hands?

_____

_____
_____
_____
_____
_____
_____
_____
_____
_____
_____
_____
_____
_____

How does my body feel when I imagine loosening the grip?

_____
_____
_____
_____
_____
_____
_____
_____
_____
_____
_____
_____

What might open if I allowed my hands to stay unclenched?

_____
_____
_____
_____
_____
_____
_____
_____
_____

_____
_____
_____
_____

Every time you catch yourself tightening again, return to this image. Whisper:
"Open hands. Open heart. Open path."

Close your eyes. Imagine one thing you've been gripping.

Now picture yourself loosening your hand, even just a little.

What emotion comes up when you imagine letting go?
Fear? Relief? Sadness? Freedom?

Write it here: _____

And now, finish this sentence:

I am safe to release _____.
And I trust that in doing so, _____. □

Check Boxes: Where Can You Soften?
□ Timing (When things happen)
□ Outcomes (How it unfolds)
□ Other people's opinions
□ Money flow
□ Family dynamics
□ My own pace

Doodle Prompt
Draw roots instead of branches. Imagine yourself like bamboo — nothing visible yet,
but something strong building underneath. Label the roots with the unseen work you're
doing now (healing, patience, trust, clarity).

Affirmations

I trust that what's meant for me doesn't need to be forced.
I am safe to release the timeline and receive the truth.
I am open to being guided in ways I can't yet see.
I don't need all the answers to take the next step.
My open hands are ready to hold miracles.

Surrender doesn't erase the unknown — it transforms it. Every time you loosen your grip, you create space for grace to land. The breakdowns, the delays, the reroutes? They're not punishments. They're positioning. Open hands. Open heart. Open path.

YOUR ORACLE PULL

Pick a number that calls to you.
Flip to the back to reveal your message.

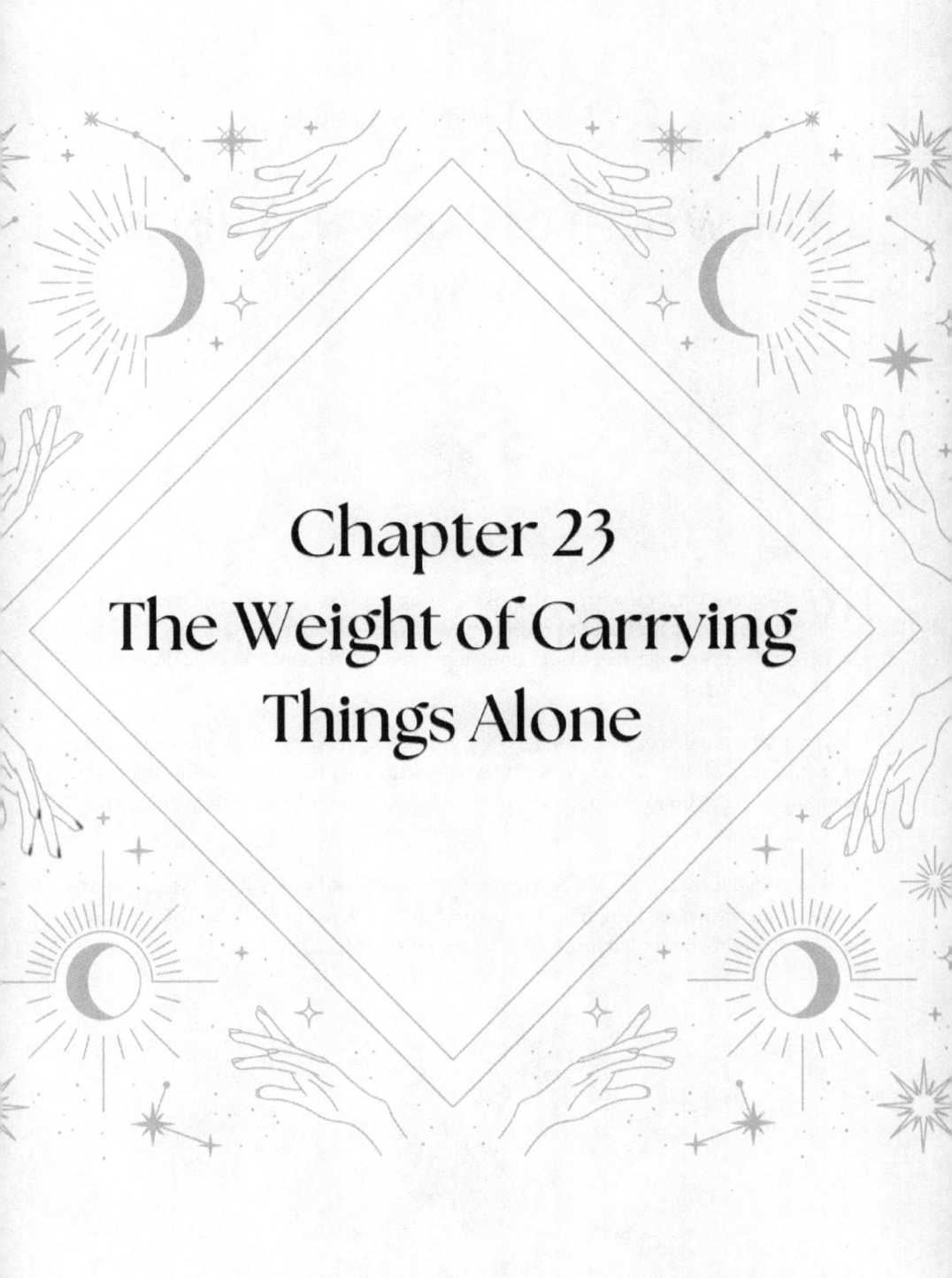

Chapter 23
The Weight of Carrying Things Alone

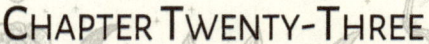

THE WEIGHT OF CARRYING THINGS ALONE

We've been taught that strength looks like carrying it all... the house, the schedule, the emotions, the fear. But real strength isn't white-knuckling your way through the weight. It's knowing when to set something down. It's remembering you don't have to hold it all alone.

This chapter reminded us that unspoken fear gets heavier in silence, that grief multiplies when hidden, and that "holding space" means presence (not fixing, not performing, not wrapping pain in a bow). Support isn't weakness. Asking for help isn't a burden. It's the bridge back to connection.

So as you step into this workbook section, let yourself be honest about what you're carrying, where you need help, and who you trust to sit with you in the dark. This is where the healing begins: not in holding it all, but in allowing yourself to be held.

What am I currently carrying that no one else knows about?

_____

_____
_____
_____
_____
_____
_____
_____
_____
_____
_____
_____
_____
_____
_____

Who in my life feels safe enough to sit with me in it, without trying to fix it?

_____
_____
_____
_____
_____
_____
_____
_____
_____
_____
_____
_____

Where have I mistaken silence for strength?

_____
_____
_____
_____
_____
_____
_____
_____
_____

_____

_____

_____

What does "holding space" mean to me — both offering it and receiving it?

_____

_____

_____

_____

_____

_____

_____

_____

_____

_____

_____

_____

If I whispered, *"This is too heavy,"* what part of me would finally exhale?

_____

_____

_____

_____

_____

_____

_____

_____

_____

_____

_____

_____

_____

_____

Fill-in-the-Blank: Permission Slips

I give myself permission to lay down

_____

I give myself permission to ask for

_____

I give myself permission to not hold

_____ alone

anymore.

Circle One: My Default Response to Pain
When I see someone hurting, I usually...
☐ Try to fix it right away
☐ Share my own story to relate
☐ Sit with them in silence
☐ Avoid it because it feels overwhelming

When I'm hurting, I usually...
☐ Withdraw and carry it alone
☐ Drop hints, hoping someone notices
☐ Overshare to release pressure
☐ Ask directly for support

Where are you pretending you're fine because you don't want to be a burden?
☐ My relationship
☐ My family
☐ My friendships
☐ My work/business
☐ My body
☐ My mental health
☐ Other: _____

Doodle Break:) look up "zentangle" for doodle inspo!

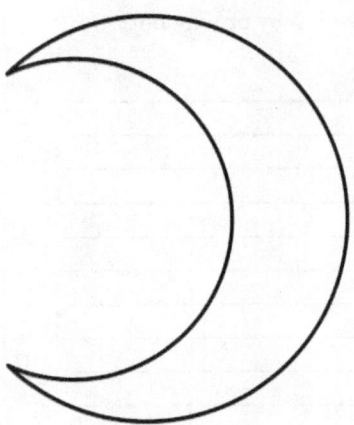

Shared Weight Practice
Use the diagram below:
In *the outer circles* write the fears, tasks, or emotions I tend to carry alone.
In *the shared circle*: write what I could invite someone else to help hold with me.

Brave Conversations: Choose one person you *trust*, and answer honestly:

Could I share what I'm carrying with them today? Why or why not?
What stops you? And what might shift if you did?

_____
_____
_____
_____
_____
_____
_____
_____
_____
_____
_____
_____
_____

_____

_____

Pattern Interrupt

When was the last time you let someone help you?
Be real...was it full surrender or a "fine, but I'll still hold most of it" kind of help?

_____

_____

_____

_____

_____

_____

_____

_____

_____

_____

_____

_____

What does asking for support look like in your life when you're not in crisis?

_____

_____

_____

_____

_____

_____

_____

_____

_____

_____

_____

_____

_____

_____

Check Boxes: Safe Ways to Be Supported
☐ Let someone listen without solutions
☐ Accept help with daily tasks (meals, errands, childcare)
☐ Say yes when someone offers support instead of saying "I'm fine"
☐ Name my need out loud, even if it feels small
☐ Choose one trusted person to tell the truth to this week

Supporting Others:

Have you ever carried someone else's grief so quietly it started to drown you?
Write what it felt like. No performance. Just truth.

_____
_____
_____
_____
_____
_____
_____
_____
_____
_____
_____
_____
_____
_____

What part of you is grieving something invisible right now?
Maybe it's the version of someone you thought you knew. Maybe it's an old dream. Maybe it's the joy you used to wake up with.

_____
_____
_____
_____
_____
_____
_____
_____
_____
_____
_____
_____
_____
_____

If you're supporting someone who's slipping under the weight—what do you wish you could say, without being afraid of saying it wrong? Say it here. Say it messy. Say it before it festers.

_____
_____
_____

_____
_____
_____
_____
_____
_____
_____
_____
_____
_____
_____

When was the last time you let yourself fall apart too? (And can you forgive yourself for it?)

_____
_____
_____
_____
_____
_____
_____
_____
_____
_____
_____
_____
_____

What would "holding space" for yourself actually look like this week?
Time? Silence? Music? Movement? Laughter? Permission to not be okay?

_____
_____
_____
_____
_____
_____
_____
_____
_____

_____
_____
_____

You are not weak. You are not too much. You are just carrying more than anyone can see. You're allowed to set it down. Even here. Even now.

Affirmations

I am worthy of support.
My vulnerability is not weakness; it is courage.
I don't have to carry everything alone.
Asking for help doesn't make me a burden; it builds a bridge.
Love expands when I let myself be seen in the heavy.

Sometimes healing isn't about getting lighter. It's about letting someone else sit in the dark with you until your own light flickers back on. You don't have to hold the whole house, the calendar, the grief, and the fear all at once. Put something down. Ask for a hand. Remember: love, real love, was built to hold weight with you.

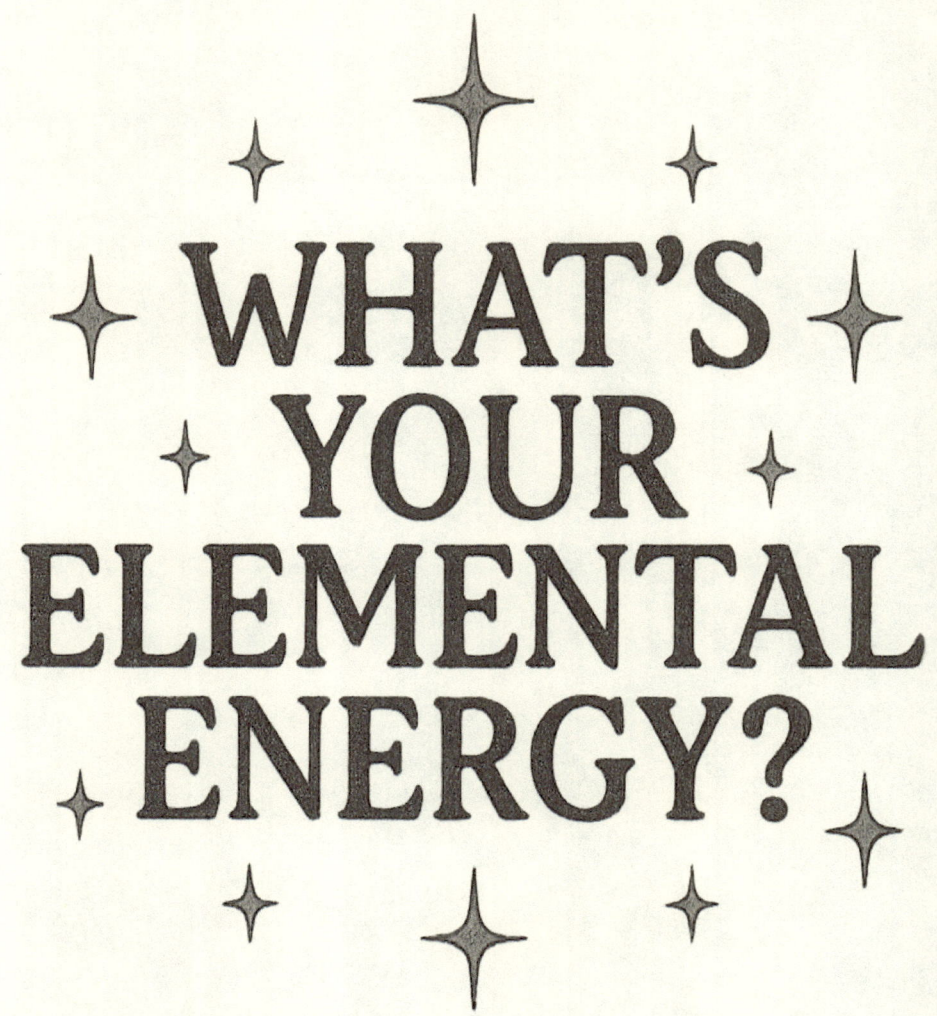

1. When life feels heavy, your first instinct is to…

a) Take action, push forward
b) Retreat and feel it all
c) Think it through, analyze from every angle
d) Ground down, focus on the practical

2. Your ideal healing ritual looks like…

a) Dancing it out, music loud
b) Journaling with tea and candles
c) Meditating under the stars
d) Gardening, cooking, or something hands-on

3. People often come to you for…

a) Motivation and courage
b) Comfort and empathy
c) Perspective and advice
d) Stability and support

4. Your shadow side sometimes shows up as…

a) Burnout or anger
b) Overwhelm or moodiness
c) Overthinking or detachment
d) Stubbornness or resistance to change

5. You feel most alive when…

a) Starting something new
b) Deep in meaningful connection
c) Exploring new ideas and possibilities
d) Building something lasting

✳ Results:

Mostly A's --> FIRE: You're blazing with passion, but remember to rest so you don't burn out.

Mostly B's --> WATER: You flow with feeling and intuition, but protect your boundaries.

Mostly C's --> AIR: You're a visionary and thinker, but don't forget to ground yourself.

Mostly D's --> EARTH: You're steady and reliable, but give yourself permission to shift and grow.

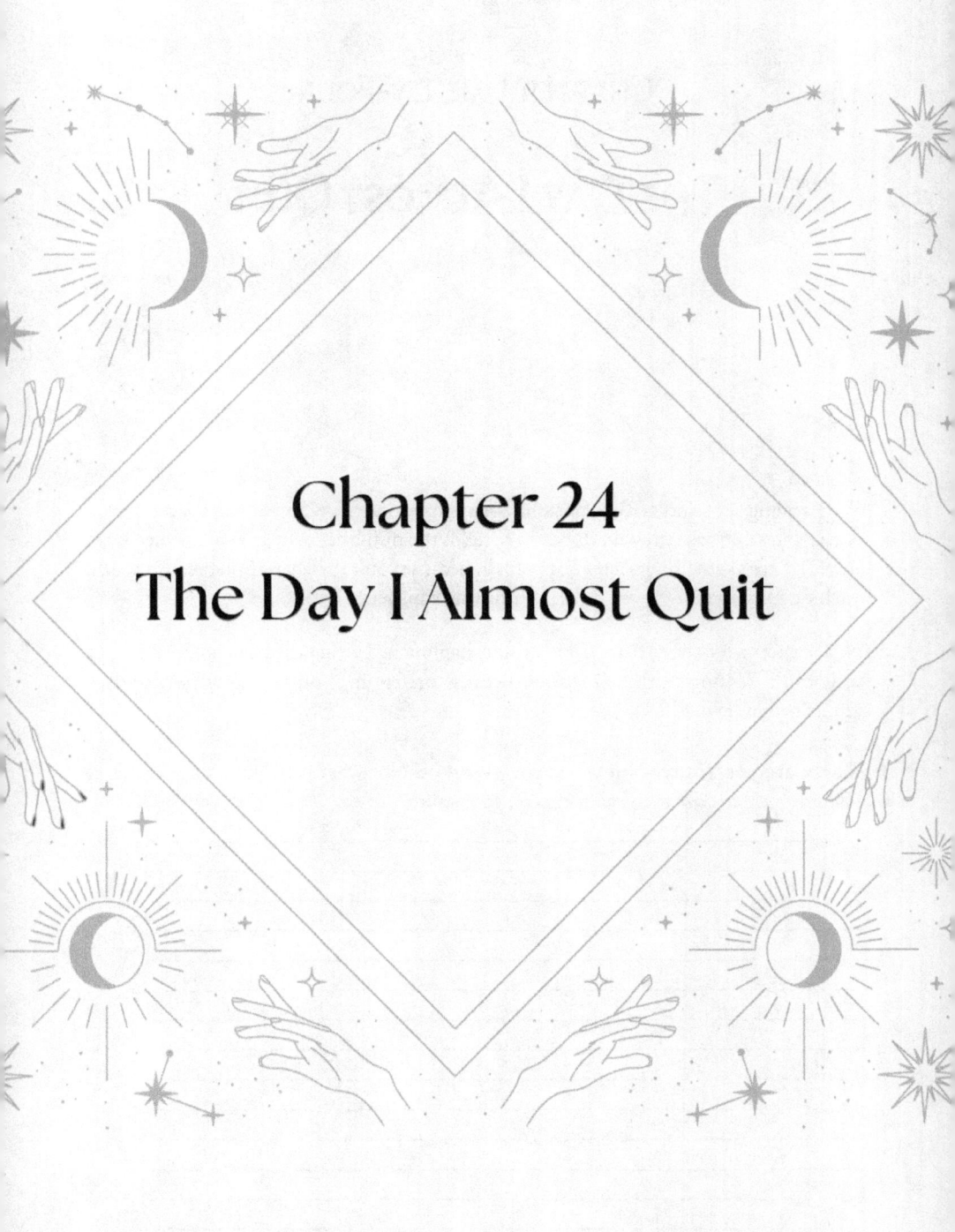

Chapter 24
The Day I Almost Quit

THE DAY I ALMOST QUIT

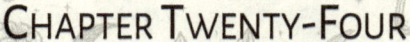

Healing isn't linear. Rock bottom doesn't have one floor. Sometimes it keeps dropping out beneath you. But even here (in the numbness, the heaviness, the "what now?") there's something sacred happening. Because you're still here. Still breathing. Still reaching for something, even if it's just one tiny whisper of hope.

This chapter isn't about fixing it. It's about naming it. Letting the page hold what your body can't. Letting truth be the tool. Because pretending you're okay is heavier than admitting you're not.

Where are you really? Not where you *should* be. Not what you'd say to a friend. But where are you in *your* body, your energy, your spirit?

_____

_____

_____

_____

_____

_____

_____

_____

_____

_____

_____

_____

_____

_____

_____

_____

Is there something you've been silently carrying that you're ready to name here? What would you say if you weren't afraid of sounding dramatic, broken, or too much?

_____
_____
_____
_____
_____
_____
_____
_____
_____
_____
_____
_____
_____

What part of this chapter cracked something open for you?

_____
_____
_____
_____
_____
_____
_____
_____
_____
_____
_____
_____
_____

What version of "rock bottom" are you trying to climb out of?

_____
_____
_____
_____
_____
_____
_____

_____
_____
_____
_____
_____
_____

What do you need to forgive yourself for right now, even if just a little?

_____
_____
_____
_____
_____
_____
_____
_____
_____
_____
_____
_____
_____

How do you define the difference between giving up and surrendering?

_____
_____
_____
_____
_____
_____
_____
_____
_____
_____
_____
_____
_____

What would it mean to stop trying to fix it, and instead just feel it?

_____
_____
_____

_____
_____
_____
_____
_____
_____
_____
_____
_____
_____
_____

What is your ocean? Your forest? Your stream? The place that could hold you today?

_____
_____
_____
_____
_____
_____
_____
_____
_____
_____
_____
_____
_____

Rock Bottom Check-In:

There are layers to rock bottom. What version of it are you in?

☐ Numbness
☐ Exhaustion
☐ Quiet rage
☐ Guilt
☐ Creative emptiness
☐ Something else: _____

The Difference Between Surrender & Giving Up: Let's explore the line between them. Complete these prompts without judgment.

Giving up feels like:

_____
_____
_____
_____
_____
_____
_____
_____
_____
_____
_____
_____
_____
_____
_____

Surrender feels like:

_____
_____
_____
_____
_____
_____
_____
_____
_____
_____
_____
_____
_____
_____
_____

Right now, I think I'm:
- ☐ Giving up
- ☐ Surrendering
- ☐ Not sure yet

Explain why:

_____
_____
_____
_____
_____
_____
_____
_____
_____
_____
_____
_____
_____
_____
_____
_____

Burn It: Sacred Release Ritual: Some truths aren't meant to live in your journal. They're meant to be witnessed...then *set free*. In the space below, write the words you need to release. Be raw. Be reckless with your honesty. Let it spill. Rage. Ache. Surrender. Then tear out this half and (safely) burn this page. Watch the smoke rise with all the heaviness you no longer owe.

_____
_____
_____
_____
_____
_____
_____
_____
_____
_____
_____
_____
_____
_____
_____
_____
_____
_____
_____
_____
_____

Affirmations

I don't have to be okay to be healing.
I can hate this part of the process and still honor it.
My softness is not weakness.
My survival is necessary.
I am allowed to pause before I rise.
Even in the pit, I am still connected to something bigger.

Gentle Reminder:

You don't need to prove your worth by pretending you're fine. Your existence in this moment, exactly as you are, is enough. Let the page hold what you can't. That's how we begin again.

Chapter 25
You're Not Too Much

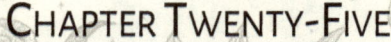

YOU'RE NOT TOO MUCH

By now, you've probably noticed the pattern: you hold more than you realize. You've carried dreams, doubts, emotions, expectations... yours and everyone else's. And still, you've kept showing up, trying to stay soft in a world that often rewards armor.

But this chapter is the reminder: you are not too much. You're not wrong for craving connection or for choosing authenticity, even when it costs you. Not everyone will meet you where you are, but that doesn't mean you shrink. It means you stay true.

Because authenticity might cost you approval, but inauthenticity costs you *yourself*. And that's too expensive.

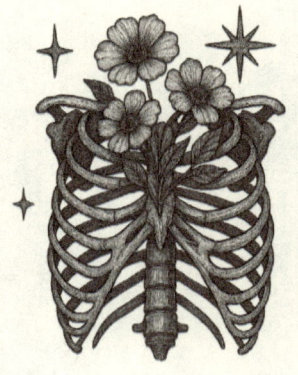

Where in your life are you still shrinking to be "palatable"?

_____

_____

_____

_____

_____

_____

_____

_____

_____

_____

_____

_____

_____

Who or what makes you feel like you're "too much"?

_____

_____

_____

_____

_____

_____

_____

_____

_____

_____

_____

_____

_____

What would it feel like to stop explaining or softening your truth?

_____

_____

_____

_____

_____

_____

_____

_____

_____
_____
_____
_____
_____

Where are you still performing vulnerability instead of living it?

_____
_____
_____
_____
_____
_____
_____
_____
_____
_____
_____
_____

What's one place in your life you're ready to stop over-giving, and simply *be*?

_____
_____
_____
_____
_____
_____
_____
_____
_____
_____
_____
_____
_____

What would it look like to let your voice, timing, and presence be enough — right now?

_____
_____
_____
_____

_____
_____
_____
_____
_____
_____
_____
_____
_____
_____
_____

Practice: The Enough Letter

Go down the page and write a letter to yourself with one simple rule: every line must end with the words *"and that's enough."*

Example:
I got out of bed today...and that's enough.
I spoke my truth, even if my voice shook...and that's enough.
I am still becoming...and that's enough."

Don't edit. Don't polish. Let it be raw. Keep writing until you feel something soften in your chest. Then read it back out loud. Let your own voice be the reminder you've been waiting for.

_____
_____
_____
_____
_____
_____
_____
_____
_____
_____
_____
_____
_____

Doodle Break: The Bridge

Check out the bridge image below. On one side, write the patterns you've been trying to leave behind (shrinking, overexplaining, people-pleasing). On the other side, write what you're moving toward (truth, integrity, alignment). In the middle of the bridge, write one word that anchors you today.

Think about someone in your life who truly "meets you in the middle." Write them a short note of gratitude (even if you don't send it). Let yourself feel what it's like to be fully seen and supported.

_____

_____

_____

_____

_____

_____

_____

_____

_____

_____

_____

_____

_____

_____

_____

You don't have to earn your place here. You don't have to perfect yourself into worthiness. The loudest rebellion you can make in a world that profits off your doubt...is to live like you are already enough. Because you are. Always have been. Always will be.

YOUR ORACLE
PULL

Pick a number that calls to you.
Flip to the back to reveal your message.

Chapter 26
The Book is Writing Us Back

THE BOOK IS WRITING US BACK

This isn't just a book you read. It's a mirror you looked into, a breadcrumb trail you followed, and a spark that pulled you closer to who you already were underneath it all. By now, you've faced your patterns, your shadows, your ego, your "not enough" stories. You've written, reflected, burned, affirmed, surrendered, and reclaimed.

And here's the wild thing, you didn't just *read* about healing. You lived it while you turned these pages. That means you're not the same person who started this. Especially as you've been writing your own story here. The hiding is over.

Who were you when you opened this book?

_____
_____
_____
_____
_____
_____
_____
_____
_____
_____
_____
_____
_____
_____
_____
_____

What was she afraid of?

_____
_____
_____
_____
_____
_____
_____
_____
_____
_____
_____
_____
_____
_____

What did she hope would change?

_____
_____
_____
_____
_____
_____
_____
_____
_____
_____
_____
_____

What weight did you finally put down? What are you no longer willing to carry forward?

_____
_____
_____
_____
_____
_____
_____
_____
_____
_____

_____
_____
_____
_____
_____

What version of yourself are you choosing to outgrow?

_____
_____
_____
_____
_____
_____
_____
_____
_____
_____
_____
_____

Where do you still hear your ego screaming "stay safe" — and what does your soul whisper back?

_____
_____
_____
_____
_____
_____
_____
_____
_____
_____
_____
_____
_____

What have you given yourself permission to want now? (Be honest. Be bold. No filtering.)
Start your answer with "I want..." and keep going.

_____
_____
_____
_____
_____
_____
_____
_____
_____
_____
_____
_____
_____
_____

What's one thing you're ready to build, choose, or live differently because of this journey?

_____
_____
_____
_____
_____
_____
_____
_____
_____
_____
_____
_____
_____

What have you built while reading this book?
— New habits?
— A shift in mindset?
— Deeper relationships?
— A softer way of speaking to yourself?

_____
_____
_____
_____
_____

_____
_____
_____
_____
_____
_____
_____
_____
_____
_____

If your life is the next chapter, what's the first line?

_____
_____
_____
_____
_____
_____
_____
_____
_____
_____
_____
_____
_____
_____
_____

Soul Tools: The Next Chapter

Scene Check → When life feels messy, ask: _Is this the scene that makes the story worth telling?_

_____
_____
_____
_____
_____
_____
_____
_____
_____
_____
_____
_____
_____

_____

_____

Pain with Purpose → Journal: *What's one thing I'm experiencing right now that's shaping me into someone stronger, softer, or more whole?*□

_____

_____

_____

_____

_____

_____

_____

_____

_____

_____

_____

_____

Live Like It's a Chapter → Ask: *If I were reading this version of me, what would I want her to do next?*□

_____

_____

_____

_____

_____

_____

_____

_____

_____

_____

_____

_____

The book may end here, but your story doesn't. The Universe didn't just call you to read these words — it called you to write the rest with your life.

Chapter 27
A Note from the Other Side

A NOTE FROM THE OTHER SIDE

This isn't a tidy bow. It's a conversation across time... a reflection on the tools that were born in the middle of the mess and how they've changed with practice. Some started as survival tactics. Some became anchors. Some reshaped entirely.

The point isn't perfection. The point is practice. You don't have to arrive. You just have to keep returning.

Pick one of the tools that resonated most with you as you read. Ask yourself:

How did I first meet this tool? (In desperation, in curiosity, in chaos, in hope?)

_____
_____
_____
_____
_____
_____
_____
_____
_____
_____
_____
_____
_____
_____

How has it changed for me now? Do I use it differently than I expected?

_____

_____
_____
_____
_____
_____
_____
_____
_____
_____
_____
_____
_____
_____

What tools do I keep in my back pocket for the foggy days?

_____
_____
_____
_____
_____
_____
_____
_____
_____
_____
_____
_____

Which ones have I outgrown, and what new ones are asking to come in?

_____
_____
_____
_____
_____
_____
_____
_____
_____
_____
_____

_____
_____
_____

What am I learning to pause for, fight for, release, or reframe now?

_____
_____
_____
_____
_____
_____
_____
_____
_____
_____
_____
_____
_____
_____

Then & Now Journal Spread

Continue the line down the middle of a page. Under *Then*, write about how you used to cope, carry, or perform in one specific area (boundaries, money, energy, authenticity, joy, etc.). Under *Now*, write about how you approach it differently today. Even if it's still messy. Even if you're still practicing.

When you're done, read both sides out loud. Let yourself feel the space you've created. That gap between *then* and *now* is proof. Proof you're becoming.

Let's bring it full circle. Answer each prompt with whatever flows...sentences, lists, even scribbles:

What tool has become your reset button? (The one you reach for when you feel off, overwhelmed, or lost.)

Which phrase from this book stuck with you? (Write it here. Then write it on a sticky note. Then put it where you'll see it.)

Where have you felt the biggest shift—in thought, behavior, or energy?

Which old belief or habit did you outgrow along the way?

What's still tender? What part of you needs patience right now?

This isn't about doing it perfectly. It's about **living what you've learned**. Put a check-mark next to any of these you've done (or want to do) *your way*:

☐ Say "we don't do that anymore" out loud when you're tempted to spiral
☐ Make a playlist just for joy
☐ Say no without apologizing
☐ Let yourself cry, journal, or pray without posting about it
☐ Delete one account, app, or person that drains your energy
☐ Take one aligned-but-illogical leap of faith
☐ Celebrate a win—without sharing it
☐ Rest before you're desperate for it
☐ Let yourself laugh, dance, or be ridiculous for no reason at all

Mirror Check: A Letter to Your Becoming

Write a note to your future self. Let it be honest. Encouraging. Grounded. Maybe even surprising.

Start with:

I don't have it all figured out, but here's what I do know...

_____
_____
_____
_____
_____
_____
_____
_____
_____
_____
_____
_____
_____
_____

You don't need to keep chasing new tools or new "fixes." You already have what you need. Integration doesn't happen in theory. It happens in practice. So don't just collect insights — _live them_. Scribble in the margins. Burn pages if you need to. Revisit what echoes. Ignore what doesn't.

You don't have to arrive. You just have to keep returning.

Chapter 28
Let Her Die
(Again and Again)

CHAPTER TWENTY-EIGHT

LET HER DIE (AGAIN AND AGAIN)

Healing doesn't end when the book does. Ego doesn't die once... she resurfaces every time you level up. The spiral is the practice. The choice is the practice. The return is the practice. This isn't about becoming someone new forever. It's about becoming *again and again*. You don't have to get it perfect. You just have to keep coming back.

Where in your life does Ego still whisper, "You're not enough" or "You're too much"?

_____
_____
_____
_____
_____
_____
_____
_____
_____
_____
_____
_____
_____
_____
_____

What does "choosing again" look like for you — not once, but daily?

_____
_____
_____

_____
_____
_____
_____
_____
_____
_____
_____
_____
_____
_____

When you imagine returning to yourself, what are the signs that you've landed?

_____
_____
_____
_____
_____
_____
_____
_____
_____
_____
_____
_____
_____
_____

Which tool from this book will you come back to first when you forget?

_____
_____
_____
_____
_____
_____
_____
_____
_____
_____
_____
_____
_____

Who do you want to be when the next dragon shows up?

_____
_____
_____
_____
_____
_____
_____
_____
_____
_____
_____
_____
_____
_____

The Spiral Is the Point

You don't just slay the dragon once. You do it again and again. And every time you rise, she returns with a new trick. List three moments from your past where you *thought* you had fully "healed", but later, a deeper layer revealed itself:

1._____

_____

_____
_____
_____

2._____
_____
_____
_____
_____

3._____
_____
_____
_____
_____

Now list one belief or behavior you *thought* you buried... that's recently come back to the surface.

What is it?:
_____
_____

Why do you think it returned now?:
_____
_____

Build a Practice of Return

Use the journal prompts below to reconnect with the version of you who *chooses* bravery, again and again:

When I'm at my boldest, I feel...
_____
_____

The version of me I'm building knows that fear isn't a stop sign, it's a signal to...
_____
_____

I recognize I'm slipping back into smallness when...
_____
_____

One thing I can do today to return to my truth is...
_____
_____
_____

Patterns of Shrinking

You said you were done hiding. And yet... the voice still shows up in subtle edits, quiet deletions, second-guessing your loudest truth.

Where do you still catch yourself shrinking to fit? *Check all that apply:*

☐ Watering down my truth to be more "palatable"
☐ Over-editing or over-explaining myself
☐ Waiting for permission to fully share
☐ Seeking outside validation before acting
☐ Pretending to be "healed" when I'm still in process
☐ Avoiding my bolder ideas out of fear they're "too much"

Pick one box you checked. What version of you is trying to survive by doing that?

_____
_____
_____
_____
_____
_____
_____
_____
_____
_____
_____
_____
_____

Anchor Reminder

"You don't just become her once. You choose her daily. And if you forget? That's okay. Come back."

Check all that apply to you today:

☐ I feel her whispering, "You're too much."
☐ I feel scared to be seen.
☐ I feel like I'm growing out of an old version of me.
☐ I feel like I'm meeting myself at a new depth.
☐ I'm choosing to rise anyway.

Recommitment Note to Self

Finish this sentence, and come back to it when you forget:

When I doubt my voice, I will remember that I've already _____. And I am becoming _____.

Soul Tool: *The Return Ritual*

This book doesn't end here. Neither does your becoming. So create a ritual of return: Choose one object that grounds you — a bracelet, a stone, a journal, a song. Every time you slip into doubt or numbness, hold that object (or play that song) and whisper: *"I choose to come back."*

Let it mark the moment you recommit... not to perfection, but to the practice. This is how you anchor yourself in the spiral. This is how you remember you're never really starting over you're just returning deeper.

You've done something brave. You didn't just read a book. You met yourself inside it. You don't get to unknow what you've seen. You don't get to pretend you're still hiding. You don't get to shrink back into the version of you who believed she wasn't ready. Because you are ready. You are becoming. And you are proof.

You made it.

H ey Beautiful,
  I am so proud of you. You made it. Even if you didn't fill out *every single part*, it doesn't matter. It was exactly as it was supposed to be. If you take nothing else from this book, take this: **You were never broken. You were never behind. You were never too much.** You don't have to earn your enoughness. You don't have to shrink yourself to be loved. You don't have to perform to be seen.

I know what it feels like to want to disappear and to want to quit. I know what it's like to wonder if maybe you're just not built for the big, bold life you keep dreaming about. I know the weight of comparison, the silence of shame, and the exhaustion of pretending. And I also know this: you're still here. Still trying. Still becoming.

That counts. More than you know.

So when the fog rolls back in, when Ego whispers in your ear, when you forget every tool you've ever underlined, don't panic. It's okay. I promise, you'll find your way back. Give yourself grace. You don't have to be fearless. You just have to be willing. Choose again. Reach for the tools, even if you can't hold them yet. Show up messy. Believe that even here, even now, the Universe is *for* you.

I can't promise you won't fall. You will. So will I. But I can promise you this: you're strong enough to rise again. Strong enough to outgrow the smallness. Strong enough to hold both the chaos and the clarity, the breakdown and the breakthrough.

And if you ever forget it, let this book remind you. Let these pages be the proof. Again, I'm proud of you. I believe in you. And I'm right here with you.

Much Love, XO
Melissa

L ast things last: a letter back to yourself. Before you close this book, pause. Meet yourself here, at the end... not the version who started these pages, but the one who finished them. The one who kept showing up, even when it was messy. The one who read, reflected, resisted, laughed, cried, grew.

Write to her.

Tell her what you've discovered about yourself along the way. Tell her what you're proud of, even if it's small. Tell her what you want her to carry forward when life gets loud again. Write the words you'll need to reread on your next Grey Day, or when Ego shows up, or when you forget just how strong you've already proven to be.

This is your mirror. Your reminder. Your evidence.
Start with:

"Hey Beautiful... look how far we've come." And let it flow.

_____
_____
_____
_____
_____
_____
_____
_____
_____
_____
_____
_____
_____
_____
_____
_____
_____
_____
_____
_____
_____
_____
_____
_____
_____

Now, go back and read that first letter. Look at her...the one who thought she had to stay small. Do you see how many dragons she's slayed since then? How many times you've laid the old version of yourself to rest? Page by page, you buried the lies, the doubt, the fear...and here you are. Seriously, take a second. That old her is gone. And now, you are unstoppable. Don't ever forget how many deaths it took to get you here and how many more it'll take you along your journey. Remember, you are exactly where you are supposed to be.

S tart with whatever flows:
   Dear Melissa... Dear Me... Dear She Who Survived...

Use these prompts if you want to go deeper:

What chapter did you *feel* more than you expected?
What truth surprised you?
What version of you did this book help lay to rest...or help rise again?
What would you say to the woman who picked this book up? And the one who finished it?

_____
_____
_____
_____
_____
_____
_____
_____
_____
_____
_____
_____
_____
_____
_____
_____
_____
_____
_____
_____
_____
_____
_____
_____
_____
_____
_____
_____
_____
_____
_____
_____
_____
_____

_____

_____

_____

_____

_____

_____

_____

_____

_____

_____

_____

_____

_____

Want to Send It for Real?

You can write this in your journal, burn it in ritual, or fold it into a keepsake drawer...
Or you can mail it to me. Not for feedback. Not for approval. Just to be _witnessed._

Find my mailing address at www.letherdie.com/mail

(You can include your return address or stay anonymous. Either way, I'll hold it with care.)

This Is a Beginning Dressed as an Ending

This book isn't finished with you, and you're not finished becoming.

Come back any time. You're always invited.

Much love, **XO**
Melissa

ONE
THE MIRROR

You are not behind – you are right on time. Every step, even the slow ones, has been carrying you forward. When doubt whispers you should be further along, look back at the ground you've already covered. You are the proof. Trust that your pace is sacred, and your timing is yours alone.

TWO
THE FLAME

Your fire will scare some people – let it. You are not here to be palatable, you are here to be powerful. Protect your spark, but don't cage it. Burn for what feels aligned, and let everything else turn to ash. The right people will warm themselves at your fire; the wrong ones were never meant to stay.

THREE
THE ROOTS

You cannot bloom without grounding. Rest is not laziness; it is a return to source. When exhaustion speaks louder than clarity, stop performing productivity and plant yourself in stillness. What feels quiet now is secretly growing strength below the surface. Honor your roots, and your next season will honor you.

FOUR
THE KEY

Not every door deserves to be opened. Some paths stay locked because they were never meant for you. Stop forcing entry where your spirit feels small. The doors meant for you won't make you beg – they'll open when you're ready. Trust your no as much as your yes, and let the right key turn with ease.

FIVE
THE WAVE

Emotions are not enemies, they're guides. Let them rise and let them move through you. Suppressing them only makes them stronger. Instead of asking, 'How do I stop feeling this?' ask, 'What is this teaching me?' Waves don't last forever, but they will carry you somewhere new if you let them move.

SIX
THE HAWK

Your signs are not coincidences – they're conversations. The hawk, the numbers, the chills, the timing... they're reminders that you're seen and supported. Stop dismissing the guidance just because it isn't logical. Spirit speaks in symbols. Trust what you notice, and follow where it points. The shift begins the moment you believe it's real.

SEVEN
THE BRIDGE

You can't drag someone across a bridge they refuse to cross. Stop shrinking, explaining, or proving to people who don't want to meet you. Some will. Some won't. That's not a reflection of your worth. Walk toward the connections that feel reciprocal, and let the rest go. Your heart deserves people who build with you, not against you.

EIGHT
THE CROWN

Your worth is not a negotiation. You don't need to earn it, explain it, or dress it up for approval. Remember: crowns aren't given, they're claimed. Wear yours daily – in your choices, your boundaries, your softness, your strength. Even in doubt, even in mess, you are still enough. Stand tall in that truth.